STUDY GUIDE

to accompany

Perry/Perry

CONTEMPORARY SOCIETY:

An Introduction to Social Science

Eighth Edition

John A. Perry

CUYAHOGA COMMUNITY COLLEGE

Erna K. Perry

LONGMAN

An imprint of Addison Wesley Longman, Inc.

New York • Reading, Massachusetts • Menlo Park, California • Harlow, England
Don Mills, Ontario • Sydney • Mexico City • Madrid • Amsterdam

STUDY GUIDE to accompany Perry and Perry: CONTEMPORARY SOCIETY: An Introduction to Social Science, Eighth Edition

Copyright © 1997 Longman Publishers USA, A Division of Addison Wesley Longman, Inc.

ISBN: 0-673-98116-9

96 97 98 99 00 9 8 7 6 5 4 3 2 1

TABLE OF CONTENTS

CHAPTER 1

THROUGH THE LENS OF SCIENCE

In this chapter, you will learn

1. of the existence of the external world, that we inherit, and the social world, that we create;
2. that the analysis of the social world with the tools of science is a fairly recent innovation;
3. the basic differences between the social and the natural sciences;
4. the elements and steps of the scientific method;
5. which disciplines constitute the social sciences;
6. the various research methods used in the social sciences.

TOPICAL OUTLINE

I. SCIENCE LOOKS AT SOCIETY
    A. The Social Sciences and the Physical Sciences Differentiated
    B. The Social World Through the Lens of Science
        1. Concepts
        2. Theories
        3. Research
            a. Variables:
                Independent and Dependent
    C. The Scientific Method
        1. Steps of the Scientific Method
            a. Selecting and defining a topic
            b. Deveoping a Research Design
            c. Verifying
            d. Generalizing
    D. The Scientific Spirit: Skepticism, Objectivity, Relativity
II. THE SOCIAL SCIENCE DISCIPLINES
    A. Anthropology
    B. Economics
    C. Geography
        1. Demography
        2. Ecology

D. History
E. Political Science
F. Psychology
G. Sociology
III. RESEARCH METHODS IN THE SOCIAL SCIENCES
   A. Sample Survey
   B. Case Studies
   C. Participant Observation
   D. Experiment
   E. Statistical Analysis
      1. Central Tendency
      2. Mean
      3. Median

A. CHAPTER OVERVIEW

The social sciences are concerned with the **social universe** that is the creation of people and results from their group way of life. Unfortunately, this social universe is difficult to analyze dispassionately and **objectively** because it involves people studying people. The **physical** sciences are more **advanced** than the social sciences because physical scientists do not let **emotion** color their research. Humans, however, cannot be studied with the same methods as inanimate objects or other animals because they cannot help but develop relationships with the subjects of their analysis.

A. FILL IN THE BLANKS:

1. The social sciences are concerned with the _Social universe_ that is a creation of people.
2. _Objectivity_ is a problem in the social sciences. _objective_
3. Physical scientists can be more _advanced_ and less _emotional_ than social scientists.
4. Humans tend to develop _relationships_ with the subjects they analyze.
5. Humans cannot be studied with the methods of the _inanimate objects / other animals_ (physical science)

B. CHAPTER OVERVIEW

The scientific method is an integral part of science and its use confers the term "science" upon any subject. The scientific method consists of a series of steps. First, the area of research must be **selected**. Second, the problem to be researched must be clearly **stated** and **defined**. Then, a **hypothesis** should be formulated. (A hypothesis is a statement of the problem and its possible solution.) The problem under investigation must then be carefully **observed**, **described**, and **recorded**. The observed data are further classified and organized to show whether there are patterns and relationships. From the above steps it is possible to **generalize** about the subject being researched. This generalization will either **validate**, **reform**, or **contradict** the hypothesis with which the researcher began research. The generalization, if the research is successfully replicated, may become a scientific **theory**. On rare occasions, if the theory explains all phenomena to which it is applied, it becomes a scientific **law**. But neither theories nor laws remain unchallenged. They are always undergoing **changes** and **revisions**.

B. FILL IN THE BLANKS:

1. An___hypothesis___is a general statement of the problem at hand and its possible solution.
2. ___Empirical_____Research___ refers to the use of human senses and precision instruments to study the subject under consideration in all its aspects.
3. Emerging patterns and relationships are shown through _____ ___Classification___and ___organization_____.
4. A formal description of the behavior of certain phenomena under specific conditions is called___Causation?___.

C. CHAPTER OVERVIEW

The social sciences include: **anthropology**, divided into **physical** anthropology, concerned with human biological origins and variation and drawing upon the natural sciences, and **cultural** anthropology dealing with preliterate societies or subgroups in their cultural variation (**archaeology** is yet another subfield of anthropology concerning itself with past societies that did not leave a written record); **sociology**, focusing on group dynamics and the forces at work when humans interact, with a stress on contemporary and mainly Western societies; **psychology**, analyzing the forces that shape and motivate individuals; **economics**, attempting to understand how societies solve the universal problem of scarcity and thus dealing with processes of supply and demand, markets, money, trade, regulation, work, etc.; **political science**, concerned with the need for government, its form, and its processes, as well as with the behavior of individuals in the political arena; **history**, which is not always studied with the scientific method, but when it is, it provides a context in which to study human relationships, as well as a sequence of related events, systematically.

Geography, which is a natural science, has features of a social science when it concerns itself with the behavior of people in a specific environment and the ways in which they use the natural environment. **Demography** (the study of population) and **ecology** (the study of the relationships between all living organisms and their natural environment) are part of geography. Even **genetics**, the science of heredity, has become important to social scientists as they try to learn about human behavior.

All of the social sciences are **interrelated** in that they all revolve around the behavior of people in social settings. The various disciplines emerged when vast amounts of information began to accumulate so rapidly that **specialization** became necessary.

C. FILL IN THE BLANKS:

1. The social science discipline that is a combination of a natural and a social science is __Anthropology__.
2. __Archaeology__ is a field of anthropology that concerns itself with historical data about past societies without a written record.
3. An emphasis on contemporary, mainly Western societies, is a feature of __sociology__.
4. In tracing the development of the newborn infant into a functioning member of society we draw upon the knowledge of the discipline of __psychology__.
5. Supply and demand, the production, distribution, and consumption of goods and services, the value of work and of natural resources are all factors examined by the discipline of __economics__.

4

6. Concepts such as the state, power, ideology and their effects on the behavior of individuals are analyzed in the context of ___political___ ___science___.

7. History is not universally considered a ___social___ ___science___.

D. CHAPTER OVERVIEW

Social scientists use such methods as **field observation** aided by **statistical data**, in-depth personal **interviews**, **case studies**, and **participant observation**. They also use **sampling techniques**, a method in which a small number of respondents represents a large population fairly accurately; **statistical correlation**, in which relationships between two or more sets of data can be established; and **probability statistics**, through which the likelihood of a result having occurred by chance can be measured. **Statistical analysis** includes descriptive statistics (mean, median, mode) that convey the central tendency--what is typical--of a group of numbers, and inferential statistics that provide the techniques researchers use to decide if they can make valid statements about a specific population based on a particular sample of it. In addition, investigators may use **in-depth analysis techniques**, detailed **personal** histories in which emotions may surface; **experiments** in which researchers interfere with natural conditions in order to find out how individuals respond in specific situations; and **simulation** models. And much of social science remains **descriptive** and cannot be definitively tested.

In the past, researchers depended to a large degree on statistical and **quantitative** ways of investigating human behavior, observing and describing social reality but not making judgments about it. Most social scientists today realize that **total objectivity** is impossible; however, they attempt to attain as much objectivity as they can.

D. FILL IN THE BLANKS:

1. Relationships between two or among more sets of data can be easily summarized through___statistical correlation___

2. The likelihood that a certain result occurs by chance is measured by___probabilrty statistics___.

3. ___Sampling___ ___Techniques___ allow a small number of respondents to represent fairly accurately large populations.

4. In the past, social scientists were expected to refrain from making ___judgment___ about social reality.

TERMS TO REMEMBER

case study: A method of research consisting of a detailed, long-term investigation of a single social unit.

concept: A generalized idea about people, objects, or processes that are related to one another; an abstract way of classifying things that are similar.

ethical neutrality: An attitude of the scientific method in the social sciences, requiring that scientists not pass moral judgment on their findings.

experiment: A method of research in which the researcher controls and manipulates variables in one group in order to test the effects of an independent variable on a dependent variable.

hypothesis: A tentative statement, in clearly defined terms, predicting a relationship between variables.

objectivity: A principle of the scientific method, especially in the social sciences, requiring researchers to divest themselves of personal attitudes, desires, beliefs, values, and tendencies when confronting their data.

participant observation: A method of research in which researchers try to take part in the lives of the members of the group under analysis, sometimes without revealing their purposes.

research: An aspect of scientific methodology that bolsters and complements theories. In the social sciences, four fundamental formats are used: the sample survey, the case study, the experiment, and participant observation.

sample survey: A method of research consisting of an attempt to determine the occurrence of a particular act or opinion in a particular sample of people.

theory: A set of concepts arranged so as to explain and/or predict possible and probable relationships.

variables: Factors whose relationships researchers try to uncover; characteristics that differ (vary) in each individual case, as opposed as to the constant, a characteristic that remains the same.

HOW MUCH DO YOU RECALL? TEST YOUR KNOWLEDGE

MULTIPLE CHOICE QUESTIONS

1. Humans are born into:
   a. a social world based on instincts
   b. environments with no pasts
   c. social worlds with traditions
   d. physical worlds created by preceding generations

2. The social sciences use methods based on:
   a. speculation
   b. artistic insights
   c. philosophies of life
   d. none of the above

3. The scientific method is based on:
   a. verification of evidence
   b. replication of scientific investigation
   c. objectivity
   d. all of the above

4. Which is not a step of the scientific method?
   a. intuition
   b. hypothesis
   c. observation and recording
   d. generalization

5. Which is not a characteristic of science?
   a. logical
   b. propositional
   c. authoritarian
   d. public

6. Science offers explanations for observations that are inexplicable by the senses alone; therefore, it is:
   a. empirical
   b. continuous
   c. self-correcting
   d. problem solving

7. The classification and organization of data:
   a. are the first step in the scientific method
   b. are called empirical research
   c. are vital because they show emerging patterns
   d. tell the scientist if a hypothesis is correct

8. Which is not exclusively a social science?
   a. geography
   b. history
   c. archaeology
   d. all of the above

9. It is easier to study physical phenomena because:
   a. they are concrete
   b. it is easier to be objective
   c. the researchers belong to the same species
   d. they are closer to the investigator

10. Which is not a method of social science research?
    a. vivisection
    b. case study
    c. sample survey
    d. participant observation

11. The Industrial Revolution brought about:
    a. the development of two new classes
    b. the migration of job seekers to cities
    c. the emergence of social sciences
    d. all of the above

12. Which is not a characteristic of scientific theory? It:
    a. explains and predicts
    b. has the force of a law
    c. is open to challenge by scientific evidence
    d. is founded on observations, concepts, and analysis

8

13. Scientific explanations are superior to common sense because:
    a. they are always subject to revision
    b. they are made by trained observers
    c. scientific observation is systematic and precise
    d. all of the above

14. Experiments:
    a. are always conducted in experimental labs
    b. are used exclusively by psychologists
    c. involve keeping all variables constant except one
    d. permit study of group culture from the inside

15. History is not entirely a social science because:
    a. historians refuse to be scientific
    b. historians study meaningful relationships
    c. history's primary object is to record human events
    d. social science is primarily concerned with the present

CHAPTER 2

IN THE BEGINNING . . .

In this chapter, you will learn

1. of the theories concerning the origin of the universe within which the planet Earth exists;
2. how life on earth began, according to the latest research findings;
3. the basic concepts, including the processes of natural selection, that comprise the theory of evolution;
4. the importance and the basic principles of genetics;
5. the historical stages of human evolution as shown by the fossil record;
6. the appearance of agriculture and its consequences;
7. the biological foundations of human culture.

TOPICAL OUTLINE

I. THE UNIVERSE
    A. Theories of How it Began
    B. The Earth and the Solar System
II. THE BEGINNINGS OF LIFE
    A. The Emergence of the Theory of Evolution
    B. A Revolution in Thought: Darwin and His Theory
    C. Natural Selection
        1. The Role of Heredity
III. GENETICS
    A. Population Genetics: Factors for Change
        1. Mutation
        2. Genetic Drift
        3. Gene Flow
        4. Speciation
        5. Natural Selection and Adaptation
IV. THE LONG TREK: HUMAN EVOLUTION
    A. From Ape to Hominid
    B. Split Between Chimpanzee and Human Lines
    C. The Road to Homo Sapiens
V. HOMO SAPIENS: MODERN HUMANS
VI. AGRICULTURE: CULTIVATION AND DOMESTICATION
VII. THE EVOLUTION OF HUMAN NATURE
    A. Biological Foundations

A. CHAPTER OVERVIEW

The universe is thought to be between 8 and 10 billion years old. According to the currently dominant theory, the **big bang** theory, it began with a gigantic explosion that was the result of a submicroscopic, infinitely dense and unimaginably hot knot of pure energy that flew outward in all directions, eventually giving rise to radiation and matter. The force of gravity then drew the matter to denser regions which, over billions of years, became galaxies, stars, planets, and everything that exists.

Life is thought to have originated in the oceans, where simple one-celled organisms developed and acquired the ability to reproduce. Growing in complexity, these organisms eventually gave rise to plants and animals. When plants could survive on dry land, the environment was ready to house living things such as huge reptiles, flying birds, and small mammals. Mammals were the most insignificant of the animals, but they were adaptable and survived great climatic changes. One order of mammals, the primates, took to a life in the trees of the thick forests that were covering the earth and began an evolutionary process that culminated in the emergence of humans.

A. FILL IN THE BLANKS:

1. The "big bang" with which the universe began is said to have occurred __8__ to __12__ _billion_ years ago.
2. Galaxies and planets were formed because of _gravity_.
3. The universe continues to _expand_.
4. Most of the universe consists of _dark_ _matter_
5. The earth is probably _2 billion_ years old.
6. In about 1.5 billion years, the sun will become _hotter_ and _melt_ the earth.
7. Life began in the form of _one-celled_ _organism_ in the oceans.
8. The organisms that fed on plants evolved into _animals_.

12

B. CHAPTER OVERVIEW

The line of development of all living creatures from one-celled microorganisms to complex beings such as modern humans is explained by the theory of **evolution**. The idea on which this theory is based--that **species** undergo **changes** to **adapt** to different environments--was not new, but it was not generally accepted because it went against the biblical explanation of creation according to which God had created a rigid hierarchy of essentially unchangeable species. The **nineteenth century**, in which many **social and cultural changes** occurred, predisposed scientists to accept the notion of change in animal species, bolstered further by the discoveries of fossils of creatures that were no longer in existence.

The **theory of evolution**, proposed by Charles Darwin in <u>The Origin of the Species</u>, posited that **species are not unchangeable**; that species belonging to the same category are **lineal descendants** of some other species that are probably extinct; and that the **mechanism** of evolutionary change is natural selection. **Natural selection** is a process in which some individuals out of a varied population are, by chance, born with traits that help them survive in a specific environment. They **pass** these traits on to some of their descendants who also flourish, **reproduce**, and transmit the successful trait. The individuals who do not possess such a trait are **less successful**, tend not to live long enough to reproduce, and thus they eventually **disappear** from the population. As the environment changes, or as individuals wander into a new environment, new traits become **adaptive** (leading to success in survival), and the process repeats itself.

The theory of evolution was further **clarified** by the work of **Gregor Mendel** who concluded that traits of two individuals who mate are **not blended**; rather, some traits are **dominant** and tend to appear in the offspring, and others are **recessive** and tend to remain hidden, although they do not disappear completely (they may reappear in future generations when two individuals with the same recessive trait mate). Even minute changes leading to an improvement in the ability to survive could, given sufficient time, result in substantial evolutionary change.

B. FILL IN THE BLANKS:

1. The theory of evolution is based on the notion that species are
   ___changeable___.
2. In the biblical account of creation, God created an immutable
   ___hierarchy___ of species
3. A more receptive attitude toward change became evident in the
   ___19th___ century.
4. Fossils of creatures that were ___extinct___ were being discovered.
5. <u>The Origin of the Species</u> is the revolutionary work of___-
   ___Charles Darwin___.
6. Evolutionary change occurs through ___Natural___ ___Sel-
   ection___.
7. Individuals who lack a trait helpful to survival in a given environment eventually become ___extinct & disappear___
8. According to Gregor Mandel, some traits are ___dominant___
   and others ___recessive___.

C. CHAPTER OVERVIEW

Evolution has been bolstered by the science that **studies heredity, genetics**, which is divided into such subfields as chromosomal, biochemical, and population genetics. According to genetics, traits are transmitted by hereditary units called **genes** which contain a blueprint with instructions for the structure of every part of every living organism. Genes are **arranged in linear order** into units called **chromosomes** which are **located** in the **nucleus** of every cell of an organism. Humans have **46 chromosomes**, one-half inherited from each parent. An individual's **genotype** consists of all the hereditary factors contained in his/her genes. An individ-ual's **phenotype** is made up of the visible, or expressed, traits. The genes themselves are made up of a complex biochemical substance called **DNA** which is the basic building block of life. Evolutionary change occurs through mutation, genetic drift, gene flow, and speciation. **Mutations** are permanent changes in genetic material; they are random and on the whole negative. **Genetic drift** occurs when a trait becomes dominant in a segment of the population because of its isolation. **Gene flow** is the movement of genes from one population to another through interbreeding. **Speciation** is the development of a new species as a result of such profound genetic changes that breeding with the original species becomes impossible. Speciation is irreversible.

C. FILL IN THE BLANKS:

1. The science that explores the mechanisms of heredity is
_____genetics_____.
2. Traits are transmitted by _____genes_____.
3. Genes are hereditary units containing an_____blueprint_____with
instructions for every part of an organism.
4. Genes are arranged in a line into _____chromosomes_____.
5. Humans have _46_ chromosomes located in the _____nucleus_____ of
every cell.
6. Each parent contributes _23_ chromosomes to the offspring.
7. All the hereditary factors contained in an individual's genes are
his/her _____genotype_____.
8. A phenotype consists of all the _____visible_____, _____external_____,
traits.
9. The basic building block of life is called _____DNA_____.
10. Evolutionary change occurs through _____mutation_____, _____genetic drift_____
_____, _____genetic flow_____ and _____speciation_____.
11. The development of a new species is
called_____speciation_____.
12. Genetic drift occurs when a segment of a population becomes
_____isolated_____.

D. CHAPTER OVERVIEW

Heredity determines **variation** in the human species. One way in
which humans vary is according to race. A **race** is a breeding
population of individuals who can be identified by the frequency
with which a number of inherited traits appears among them. The
reason for the frequency of some traits in a given breeding population is probably **isolation**, which has created a limited gene
pool--not enough individuals with new traits. The term "race" has
been greatly misused and misunderstood primarily because people
attribute to the different races **socially** significant differences,
whereas the differences are **purely physical**. This faulty
connotation originated in the 18th century, which was one of territorial expansion for many white-skinned peoples; thus, ideas of
superiority and inferiority became confused with physical differences that are **adaptations** to a **specific environment** at a certain
stage of a population's evolution. There are a number of breeding
populations in existence today, but it is impossible to state how
many races there are because that number varies according to
how one classifies who belongs to which race. If one uses skin

15

color, one gets one number; but if one uses eye shape one gets another. Thus, **scientists classify** populations into very **broad categories**: Mongoloid, Negroid, and Caucasoid. Individuals in these categories vary not only in appearance, but also in some **biochemical factors**, such as the type of ear wax, blood type, and fingerprint patterns. But geneticists agree that there is much more **variety within** a racial group than **between** racial groups. **All humans belong to the same species**, and no speciation has taken place; there are an extraordinary number of overlapping variations within human breeding populations, so that we are all **hybrids**.

D. FILL IN THE BLANKS:

1. Variation in the human species occurs as a result of heredity.
2. A breeding population whose members are identified by the frequency with which inherited traits appear among them is a race.
3. Isolation can result in an limited gene pool.
4. "Race" has been misused and misunderstood because it refers to physical differences among people, not social ones.
5. The misunderstandings began in the l8th century which was an era of expansionism for Western nations.
6. The physical differences visible in members of different races are due to adaption to a certain environment at some point in evolution.
7. The number of races depend on the way populations are____-classified.
8. The broad categories into which breeding populations are divided by scientists are Negroid, Mongoloid, and Caucasoid.
9. Racial groups vary in outward appearance but also in biochemical factors.
10. Geneticists agree that we are all hybrids and there are more differences within racial groups than between them.

E. CHAPTER OVERVIEW

One order of **mammals**, the **primates**, began living in trees some 70 million years ago when the earth was covered by forests. Eventually, these primates, called prosimians (ape-like) by anthropologists, developed a fine **grasping mechanism** consisting of hands with fingers and an opposing thumb to hold unto branches; **eyes** in

16

the front of the head for better vision; and a complex **cerebral cortex** to coordinate behavior. About 35 million years ago, the prosimians diversified into monkeys and a little later into apes. Some of these apes eventually attempted to live on the ground. The evolution of modern humans did **not** occur in a **straight line**; rather, more than one group of hominids existed side by side. But, approximately one million years ago only one hominid group remained, called <u>Homo erectus</u> (the upright human), the ancestor of our own species, <u>Homo sapiens</u> (the wise human). <u>Homo sapiens</u> fossils date back 75,000 years ago. Among them are those of the **Neanderthals** who provided the stereotype of the "caveman," and the **Cro-Magnon**, dating from between 30,000 to 35,000 years ago, who belonged to the same species modern humans do. These humans survived primarily through **hunting and gathering** until the invention of agriculture.

Agriculture first appeared in the Near East in an area bordering the Persian Gulf, spread to southeastern Europe about 8000 years ago, and northward and westward for the next 15 to 20 centuries. It brought with it **permanent settlements**, **cities**, and the **domestication of animals**. It also led to surpluses, warfare, and great **population growth**.

E. FILL IN THE BLANKS

1. Extinction is the result of a failure to _adapts_.
2. Mammals originated about _225_ million years ago.
3. Primates are an order of _mammals_.
4. Life in the trees forced the prosimians to develop an_grasping_ -_mechanism_, better _vision_, and a complex _cerebral cortex_.
5. The prosimians are the predecessors of _moneys_ and _apes_.
6. Several groups of hominids lived _side by side_.
7. Homo erectus is a precursor of _Homo sapiens_.
8. Fossils dating back 30,000 to 35,000 years are attributed to the _Cro-Magnon_.
9. Agriculture first appeared in an area called the _Fertile Crescent_ in the _Near East_.

17

F. CHAPTER OVERVIEW

At the same time that humans were **evolving biologically**, they were also developing **customs and habits** that helped them survive in their environment, and that differentiated them from other animals. It is important to remember that biological realities have **social consequences**. Thus, humans probably began walking on two feet (bipedalism) for a number of reasons, at first probably only because it helped them see as they walked in the tall grass. But the fact that they **walked on two feet** had a number of very important **social results**: the use of their hands enabled them to carry food from place to place and to manipulate objects with tools. These tasks made them more intelligent, enlarging their brain. **Large-brained infants** must be born small and immature in order to pass through the mother's birth canal. Such infants require a long period of care and are **dependent on an adult**. A mother caring for a dependent infant is not an effective provider; thus, she may have sought the **protection of a male**, leading to a rudimentary **family bond**. Other **social processes** emerged from the mechanisms of **biological adaptation** among which were probably **cooperation** and sharing, the **incest taboo**, a simple **moral system**, as well as such feelings as gratitude, sympathy, friendship, guilt, shame, and moral indignation. When groups of humans had grown large in size and complexity, a certain degree of **organization** became necessary, causing the emergence of **troops** with leaders and hierarchies of dominance, and eventually **tribes** and tribal unions with an ever-increasing number of rules and procedures.

Progress in the development of **social systems** was much enhanced by the discovery and subordination of fire that allowed humans to wander much farther into colder climates; to protect themselves from predators, and to live in caves. Indirectly, fire also contributed to **reshaping** the contours of the human face, to increasing the **complexity** of language, to producing feelings of **community**, and to the emergence of **religion**. In short, what we call "human nature," as well as "culture," or the way of life of people, were developing alongside human biological evolution.

F. FILL IN THE BLANKS:

1. Biological realities have _____social_____ consequences.

2. Dependent infants force their mothers to become dependent on _males_.

3. Some of the social processes that emerged from the biological change to bipedalism were _cooperation_, _sharing_, and _incest taboos_.

4. When groups of humans grew large they had to submit to various levels of _organization_.

5. Living in colder climates and in caves, defending themselves from predators, and eating cooked food followed the discovery of _fire_.

TERMS TO REMEMBER:

australopithecus: The fossil remains of a prehuman who lived from abound 5 million to 1.5 million years ago. Some researchers maintain that this type of prehuman is not a direct ancestor of modern humans, but rather is a contemporary of an upright-- walking, meat-eating, large-brained species that survived; others insist that Australopithecus is on the human ancestral line.

chromosomes: Carriers of genes, or the hereditary blueprints of organisms. Each human inherits a set of 23 chromosomes from each parent.

cro-magnon: Fossil remains of the closest predecessors of modern humans who lived about 35,000 years ago. They were expert tool makers and artists, and lived in tribes that displayed evidence of rules and kinship systems.

dna: Deoxyribonucleic acid. A complex biochemical substance (protein) that is the basic building block of life. It determines the inheritance of specific traits.

estrus: Period of sexual receptivity and ability to conceive.

evolution: A theory that explains change in living organisms and variation within species. Evolution functions according to processes of natural selection, mutation, genetic drift, gene flow and speciation.

gene flow: The movement of genes from one gene pool to another. It results in new combinations of genes in the offspring.

gene frequency: The proportion in which the various genes occur in an inbreeding population.

gene pool: All of the genetic material available to a population to be inherited by the next generation.

genes: Hereditary units that transmit an individual's traits. They are contained in the chromosomes and made up of DNA.

genetic drift: The fluctuations in frequencies of specific traits in a small, isolated population, so that visible differences between an isolated population and the population from which it broke away become obvious.

genetics: The science of heredity.

hominids: Prehuman creatures who walked on two feet.

homo erectus: The upright hominid thought to be a direct ancestor of modern humans.

homo sapiens: A species whose fossils date back 75,000 years and include Neanderthal. The species label for modern humans is Homo sapiens sapiens, whose fossils date back 30,000 years and include Cro-Magnon.

mutation: A permanent change in genetic material.

natural selection: A process of evolution in which random traits are tested for their survival value; the successful traits are passed on, while organisms possessing less successful traits eventually become extinct.

neanderthal: A subspecies of Homo sapiens whose fossil remains date from 70,000 to 35,000 years ago. They are known to have buried their dead.

primates: An order of mammals to which monkeys, apes, and humans belong.

ramapithecus: A hominoid having hominid-like features, dated between 8 and 14 million years ago.

HOW MUCH DO YOU RECALL? TEST YOUR KNOWLEDGE

MULTIPLE CHOICE QUESTIONS

I. According to the "big bang" theory, the universe:
   a. began with a hot knot of pure energy
   b. continues to expand
   c. is between 8 and 12 billion years old
   d. all of the above

2. Life originated:
   a. in the Far East
   b. in the oceans
   c. on dry land
   d. in the atmosphere

3. Prosimians:
   a. were the ancestors of monkeys, apes, and humans
   b. were mammals
   c. took to life in trees
   d. all of the above

4. Hominids are primates that have:
   a. locomotion on two feet
   b. comparatively large brains
   c. non-protruding faces
   d. all of the above

5. According to anthropologists:
   a. more than one group of hominids lived side by side
   b. humans evolved in a straight line of development
   c. hominids are the ancestors of contemporary apes
   d. humans are descended from the great apes of Africa

6. Along with biological changes, social processes like the following were also emerging:
   a. monogamy
   b. cooperation and sharing
   c. bipedalism
   d. larger brains

7.   Which was **not** a result of the discovery of fire?
     a. a new shape for the human face
     b. progress in the development of language and religion
     c. ability to wander further into colder climates
     d. hunting and gathering

8.   According to Charles Darwin, the primary mechanism of evolutionary change is:
     a. cross breeding
     b. natural selection
     c. hybridization
     d. phenotype

9.   The hereditary units that transmit traits and characteristics are called:
     a. DNA
     b. genotypes
     c. phenotypes
     d. genes

10. Differences among racial groups include:
     a. variation in blood type
     b. biochemical factors
     c. cultural factors
     d. only a and b

11. The discovery of two 350,000-year-old skulls in China suggests that:
     a. modern humans may have developed independently in various parts of the world
     b. the African origin of Homo Sapiens is a hoax
     c. Homo Sapiens and Homo Erectus are both hominids
     d. all of the above

12. The earliest **hard evidence** of Homo Sapiens in the New World:
     a. goes back to 40,000 B.C.
     b. goes back 12,000 years
     c. goes back 5,000 years
     d. none of the above

22

13. Genetics is concerned with:
    a. how chromosomes transmit genes across generations
    b. the reasons for genetic variations and changes in populations
    c. biochemical and cellular events
    d. all of the above

14. Genetic flow entails:
    a. permanent change in genetic material
    b. the movement of genes from one breeding population to another
    c. the evolution of one species into another
    d. all of the above

15. The loss of estrus in human females:
    a. lessened competition among males for females
    b. built stronger bonds between specific males and females
    c. provided children with two protective adults
    d. all of the above

CHAPTER 3

CULTURE: PRODUCT AND GUIDE TO LIFE IN SOCIETY

In this chapter, you will learn

1.   why humans are unique;
2.   the importance of symbols;
3.   the importance of shared meanings;
4.   why culture is responsible for all human progress;
5.   what culture consists of;
6.   why norms are vital to societies;
7.   the difference between the attitudes of ethnocentrism and
      cultural relativity;
8.   of the existence of subcultures and countercultures.

TOPICAL OUTLINE

I. CULTURE
      A. Biological Predispositions to Culture
      B. The Birth of Culture
      C. Cultural Evolution and Sociobiology
      D. What Is Culture?
      E. The Symbolic Nature of Culture
            1. The Necessity of Sharing Symbols
II. THE MOST IMPORTANT SYSTME OF SYMBOLS:
      LANGUAGE
      A.   Does Language Create Reality?
III. THE CONTENT OF CULTURE
      A. Material Culture
      B. Nonmaterial Culture
      C. Components of Nonmaterial Culture: Cognitive and
      Normative
IV. THE NORMATIVE SYSTEM
      A. Values
      B. Norms
            1. Imperfect Agreement
            2. Social Integration
      C. Categories of Norms
            1. Folkways
            2. Laws
            3. Mores

A. CHAPTER OVERVIEW

Humans' **biological makeup** predisposes them to **develop culture**. For instance, among primates humans alone are completely **bipedal**. Human hands with the opposing thumbs are ideal for grasping, holding, and manipulating even the smallest and most delicate object. Humans' eyes face forward, enabling them to operate together in a stereoscopic manner that allows people to judge distances accurately, and to see objects three-dimensionally and in color. Humans also have a brain of massive size in proportion to the body that is much more complex in structure and function than that of any other animal. This complex brain enables humans to remember, think abstractly, and symbolize, qualities that seem to be uniquely human. A speech center in the brain also enables humans to use their vocal cords for speaking and communicating with one another. The above are **biological advantages**. But humans must also overcome a number of **disadvantages** in the quest for survival. First, humans are much weaker than many animals, lacking the latters' sharp teeth or claws. Then, the human infant is completely helpless and requires a long period of maturation. Finally, humans lack instincts and inborn patterns of behavior; thus, they must learn how to behave in the most advantageous manner.

A. FILL IN THE BLANKS:

1. A predisposition toward the development of culture may be found in humans' _biological_ _makeup_.
2. Human hands are especially adept at _grasping_, _holding_, and _manipulating_.
3. Stereoscopic vision enables people to _judge distances_ accurately and see objects _3-dimensionally_ and in color.

26

4. The human _____brain_____ is much larger and more complex than that of other animals.

5. The most important functions of the human brain are the abilities to _think_ _abstractly_, _remember_, and _symbolize_.

6. A speech center in the brain allows people to _communicate_ with each other.

7. Among human biological disadvantages are _weakness_, a long period of infancy, and lack of _instinct_.

B. CHAPTER OVERVIEW

Culture is a frequently misunderstood term. In a general way, culture **is the way of life of a people**. More specifically, culture is **a product** of **social interaction**; it **includes** all the accumulated **knowledge**, ideas, **values**, goals, and **material objects** of a society; it is **learned** by each member of a society during **socialization** (the process of becoming human); it **provides individuals** with ways of satisfying **biological and emotional** needs through patterns and systems of organized behavior. Each culture is **distinct** from every other culture, but all cultures share important **similarities**. Finally, cultures are always in a state of change. Culture is possible because humans can communicate by means of **symbols**, rather than through **signals** as animals do. Signals are biologically determined and genetically transmitted, so they cannot be taught. Symbols are signs that can be taught; they are abstractions that stand for realities whose meanings are agreed upon by all members of a group. The most effective **system of symbols** is **language**, although **gestures, music, and art** are also symbol systems. Language is the most significant product of culture, and is at the same time the foundation on which culture is further developed and transmitted. Language allows people to create the dimensions of time and space, and, through writing, to expand knowledge and allow it to accumulate. Language and culture are so interrelated that if a culture does not value a certain trait, there is no word for it in that culture, and people are not aware that such a trait exists. Language, then, **shapes reality**. However, the potential for acquiring language is innate and universal in humans everywhere.

B. FILL IN THE BLANKS:

1. Culture is the product of _social_ _interaction_.

2. Culture includes all the _knowledge_, _ideas_, _values_, _goals_, and material objects of a society.

3. Culture is transmitted during the process of _socialization_.

4. _Socialization_ is learning to become human.

5. Culture allows people to satisfy biological and emotional needs through creating _patterns/systems_ of _behavior_.

6. Symbols make _culture_ possible.

7. Animals communicate through _signals_ that are biologically determined and _genetically_ transmitted.

8. The most effective system of symbols is _language_ although _gesture_, _music_ and art are also symbol systems.

9. Language is the most significant product of culture: it allows culture to be _transmitted_; knowledge to be accumulated; and the dimensions of space and time to be _created_.

10. Language shapes _reality_ because if we cannot say it, it does not exist.

C. CHAPTER OVERVIEW

Culture may be divided into a **material** and a **nonmaterial** component. The material component consists of all the products conceived and manufactured by humans from the beginning of time to the present. **Nonmaterial culture** consists of abstractions that include **knowledge, beliefs, values, and rules for behavior**. The two components cannot exist apart from one another. Nonmaterial culture may be further divided into a symbolic component (language), a cognitive component (knowledge, beliefs, technology) and the normative component (values, norms--folkways, mores, laws--institutions, and sanctions). The **normative system** is the most significant because it **explains** why **societies work as they do**. It consists of difficult to define abstractions, called values, which are evaluations as to what is good, right, moral, beautiful, or ethical, and thus desirable. **Norms are rules** that tell people how to act, think, or feel on given occasions. Norms that specify expected behavior in everyday, **commonplace** situations are termed **folkways**, a term coined by William Graham Sumner. Norms that prescribe behavior in **important** matters are called **mores**. Mores define the rightness of wrongness of an act and their violation is considered a crime against society. **Taboos** are mores prohibiting certain acts considered extremely repellent such as murder, incest, cannibalism. **Laws** are **formal codes of behavior** binding on **every member of society**. They specify what constitutes deviation and punishment for it. Norms are internalized by most people, becoming their "conscience," but laws are not--they are needed in a complex, heterogeneous society where norms are not fully accepted by all. The reason for the importance of the normative system is that in a group setting most members must conform most of the time in order to avoid chaos and anarchy. A society must exert a degree of **social control**, and it does it through the normative system that is more effective than force or coercion. Norms are enforced through **sanctions** that are divided into rewards (**positive** sanctions) or punishment (**negative** sanctions), and that can be **official** (positive: public recognition; negative: jailing) or **unofficial** (positive: a pat on the back; negative: being avoided or yelled at). Norms are also followed by most people because we have a strong need to belong to a group and do not like being outcasts. Norms, however, are not universally obeyed: some people never learn them, and others break them knowingly. In addition, some norms in society represent **ideal** behavior that most people, in reality do not follow. Cultural norms refer to ideal norms, whereas when speaking about how people really behave, we use **statistical** norms.

C. FILL IN THE BLANKS:

1. The two chief divisions of culture are into
   ___material___ and ___non material___.
2. All objects conceived and manufactured by humans from the beginning of human existence to the present are part of
   ___material___ ___culture___.
3. Abstractions such as knowledge, beliefs, values, and rules of behavior are part of ___non material___ ___culture___.
4. Nonmaterial culture has a symbolic, cognitive, and ___norma-tive___ _____component.
5. The normative system consists of ___values___,
   ___norms___, ___institutions___, ___sanctions___.
6. Evaluations as to what is good, moral, beautiful and ethical are called ___values___.
7. Rules that tell people how to think, act, or feel on specific occasions are ___norms___.
8. Norms may be further subdivided into ___folkways___,
   ___mores___, ___taboos___, and ___laws___.
9. Laws are needed in complex societies because ___norms___ are not fully accepted by all.

29

10. The normative system is important because in a group setting most individuals must ___conform___ most of the time to avoid chaos.

11. Conformity to norms is achieved mainly by a system of positive and negative, official and unofficial ___sanctions___.

12. People also conform to norms because they have a strong need to ___belong___.

D. CHAPTER OVERVIEW

Since culture is a **patterned system of behavior**, for the sake of analysis its structure can be further broken down. The smallest element or unit of culture is a **trait**. A number of traits that accumulate around an activity is a **culture complex**. And a number of culture complexes clustering around a central human activity becomes an **institution**. Thus, a football helmet would be an element of material culture, team spirit and a belief in winning would be elements of nonmaterial culture, the game of football would be a culture complex, and sport would be an institution in American culture. Institutions are **formal systems of beliefs** and behavior composed of **interrelated norms and culture complexes** centering primarily on the five most **pressing human needs**: to provide food and shelter, to regulate sex and continue the species, to maintain peace and order, to transmit culture to each new generation, to explain the unknown and give purpose to human life. These needs have given rise to the so-called five **pivotal institutions**: the family, the economy, government, education, and religion. Institutions provide ready-made solutions as to how to satisfy these needs.

D. FILL IN THE BLANKS:

1. The smallest element or unit of culture is called an ___trait___.

2. A number of traits accumulating around an activity is an ___culture complex___.

3. Several culture complexes clustering around a central human activity is an ___institution___.

4. Institutions emerged to offer solutions to ___pressing human needs___

5. The need to regulate sex and continue the species gave rise to the institution of the ___family___.

6. The five most pressing needs resulted in the emergence of the ___pivotal___ institutions.

E. CHAPTER OVERVIEW

In traveling, it is easy to observe that societies and their cultures differ among themselves. There is a tendency for people to use the viewpoint of **ethnocentrism** that is an attitude of passing sentence on other societies according to the standards of one's own. All societies exhibit a degree of ethnocentrism; but when it becomes exaggerated it leads to misunderstanding and conflict. To counteract ethnocentrism, social scientists originated the concept of **cultural relativity**. According to cultural relativity, each culture is analyzed on its own terms, in the context of its own societal setting, without applying any universal norms or moral absolutes. Cultural **variation** has been explained on the basis of race and geography, but neither explanation is totally satisfactory. However, while variation is common and sometimes striking, there is also a great deal of similarity among cultures, that proves our common humanity.

Similarities common to all cultures are called cultural **universals**. Not only do societies share cultural universals, but they adopt one another's cultural elements, thus leading to change. When two societies meet, a mutual transmission of cultural traits, complexes, and patterns of behavior usually occurs, a process called **diffusion**. Other processes causing change in societies and their cultures include **discoveries** (introducing formerly unknown elements), **inventions** (new patterns created from existing elements of culture), and **planning**. If changes occur too rapidly, people have no time to adjust and a situation called **cultural lag** occurs. This is an inconsistency in the cultural fabric of a society that can create problems. In general, human cultures have survival mechanisms that have worked rapidly and efficiently to adapt humans to environmental changes.

E. FILL IN THE BLANKS:

I. Passing judgment on other societies according to the standards of one's own society is called _ethnocentrism_.
2. To counteract the negative effects of ethnocentrism, the concept of _cultural_ _relativity_ was suggested by social scientists.

31

3. According to cultural relativity, no __universal__ _____norms_____ nor ___moral___ ___absolutes___ should be used to judge another culture.
4. Similarities shared by all cultures are called __cultural__ __universals__.
5. Change in societies occurs through __diffusion__.
6. Additional processes of change include __invention__, __discovery__, and __planning__.
7. In a situation of cultural lag, people have no __time__ to __adjust__ to change.

F. CHAPTER OVERVIEW

Uniformities and variations occur among the various groups that make up each society. This is especially true in contemporary societies that are **heterogeneous** because members are immigrants, or occupationally specialized. A group that has distinctive features that set it apart from the wider culture of the society, yet retains the principal features of the general culture, is called a **subculture**. The term does not imply any inferiority to the culture at large; it simply distinguishes a subdivision of it. Subcultures originate because of racial and ethnic backgrounds of people, because of religion, because of specific occupations, and even around certain institutions, such as the military or government. Some groups in a society adopt a value system and goals that are in direct opposition to those of the larger culture. Such groups are not simply subcultures. They are considered **countercultures**. The basic difference between subcultures and countercultures is their attitude toward society. Subcultures for the most part reinforce the cultural values of the larger society while giving loyalty to a smaller group within it; countercultures reinforce their members' rejection of the goals, values, and norms of the larger society.

F. FILL IN THE BLANKS:

1. Uniformities and variations do not appear among societies alone, but __within__ them as well.
2. Contemporary societies tend to be __heterogeneous__ because members come from different backgrounds and are occupationally specialized.
3. A group with distinctive features but with the same values and goals as the wider society is called an __sub culture__.

32

4. Subcultures develop around _race_,
religion, _nationality_, _occupation_,
and certain institutions.
5. The term subculture does not imply any _inferiority_.
6. A group that rejects the society's values, goals, and norms
is called an _counterculture_.

TERMS TO REMEMBER

counterculture: A group that possesses a value system and goals that are in direct opposition to those of the larger society.

cultural relativity: An attitude of judging each culture on its own terms and in the context of its own societal setting.

cultural universals: Similarities common to all cultures. (Example: the existence of pivotal institutions.)

culture: The way of life of people in a society. The totality of all that is learned and shared by the members of a society through their interaction. The product of social interaction and a guide for further interaction. Culture includes material and nonmaterial aspects.

culture complex: A number of related traits that accumulate around a specific human activity.

culture trait: The smallest element or unit of culture. In material culture, it is any single object. In nonmaterial culture, it is any single idea, symbol, or belief.

ethnocentrism: The attitude that one's own culture is right and that cultural patterns different from it are wrong.

folkways: Norms that direct behavior in everyday situations; customary and habitual ways of acting.

institution: A number of culture complexes clustering around a central human activity.

laws: Formal codes of behavior. Laws are binding on the whole society; they outline behavior that deviates from the norm and prescriptions for punishing it.

mores: Norms that direct behavior considered either extremely harmful or extremely helpful to society. They define the rightness or wrongness of an act, its morality or immorality. Violation of mores is punished by society.

normative system: A system of rules regulating human behavior.

norms: Behavioral standards that dictate conduct in both informal and formal situations; a set of behavioral expectations.

sanctions: Rewards (positive) or punishments (negative) directed at individuals or groups by either legal and formal organizations (official) or the people with whom one interacts (unofficial) to encourage or discourage specific types of behavior.

signals: Biologically determined and genetically transmitted responses to outside stimuli.

social control: The process by which order is maintained within society through obedience to norms--folkways, mores, taboos, and laws.

subculture: A group that has distinctive features which set it apart from the culture of the larger society but that still retains the general values of mainstream society.

symbols: Genetically independent responses to stimuli. Symbols are learned and can be changed, modified, combined, and recombined in an infinite number of ways. Language, music, and art are common symbol systems.

taboos: Mores stated in negative terms. They center on acts considered extremely repellent to the social group.

HOW MUCH DO YOU RECALL? TEST YOUR KNOWLEDGE.

MULTIPLE CHOICE QUESTIONS

1. "The way of life of a people" is a partial definition of:
    a. a social system
    b. society
    c. culture
    d. tradition

2. Culture:
    a. is the largest social system
    b. includes abstract and concrete factors
    c. is the same in each society
    d. is found among animals as well as among humans

3. The principal difference between people and other animals is that:
    a. animals are larger and stronger
    b. people communicate with symbols while animals communicate with signals
    c. biology dictates human behavior while instincts direct animal behavior
    d. people live in families while animals live in troops

4. Symbols are:
    a. signs whose meanings are communally agreed upon
    b. biologically determined signals to outside stimuli
    c. musical instruments used to convey dramatic emotion
    d. expressions of instincts in humans

5. The birds and the bees behave in specific ways because:
    a. they have their own culture
    b. they learned by observation
    c. they are guided by instincts
    d. they are responding to a natural law

6. The most important element in the development of culture is:
    a. cooperation
    b. group activities
    c. a warning system
    d. language

7. Language is a significant invention because:
    a. it makes possible a wide range of communication
    b. it has allowed people to create the dimensions of time and space
    c. it has extended the range of knowledge of the individual
    d. all of the above

8. The cognitive component of culture:
    a. includes knowledge, beliefs, and technology
    b. is made up of rules for behavior
    c. consists of values and morals
    d. is part of material culture

9. "They designate any standard or rule that states what human beings should or should not think, say, or do under given circumstances" is a definition of:
    a. values
    b. mores
    c. beliefs
    d. norms

10. The normative system includes all **but** the following:
    a. values
    b. technology
    c. institutions
    d. sanctions

11. Folkways may be defined as:
    a. those norms derived from tradition
    b. folk wisdom transmitted through the generations
    c. norms that specify expected behavior in everyday situations
    d. norms that specify expected behavior in special, unique situations

12. Social control in society is exerted through:
    a. force
    b. the people's desire to belong
    c. sanctions
    d. all of the above

13. Traits, complexes, and institutions make up:
    a. social structure
    b. culture
    c. society
    d. statistical norms

14. Which is not a pivotal institution of society?
    a. the economy
    b. education
    c. the family
    d. a hospital

15. Which of the following groups may be considered a counter-culture?
    a. a gang of delinquent youths
    b. the Branch Davidians
    c. the Manson family
    d. all of the above

16. When we refer to how people really behave:
    a. we use statistical norms
    b. we refer to the ideal norms
    c. we speak of mores
    d. we use folkways

17. Ethnocentrism refers to:
    a. an attitude with which members of one society judge another society according to their own standards
    b. the attitude that cultures be analyzed on their own terms
    c. the attitude that certain values and practices are common to all cultures
    d. all of the above

18. "Feng shui" refers to:
    a. culture shock
    b. superstitions peculiar to the Chinese
    c. cultural superiority
    d. commerce among the Chinese

19. Individualism includes the following notions:
   a. that if each individual pursues his or her own interest, the public good automatically emerges
   b. the reaction to utilitarian individualism symbolized by the abandonment of the pursuit of wealth in favor of self-cultivation
   c. the belief that the New World was a place where the individual could get ahead on his or her own initiative
   d. all of the above

20. Pivotal institutions:
   a. arise from fundamental human needs
   b. include government, the economy, education, the family, and religion
   c. differ in traits and culture complexes from society to society
   d. all of the above

CHAPTER 4

INTERACTION: FROM TWO TO MILLIONS

In this chapter, you will learn that

1. humans are group animals who achieve survival and acquire their human nature as a result of being members of one group or another;
2. within each group, individuals are assigned statuses and carry out roles, a condition that makes of each group a social system;
3. the existence of a social system gives life predictability, so that each social situation does not continually have to be resolved anew;
4. there is a multitude and variety of groups, but that primary groups are those most important to the individual;
5. the largest group to which people belong is society;
6. there has been a trend away from the small, traditional societies of the past (Gemeinshafts) to the large associational societies (Gesellschafts) of the present;
7. the interaction that occurs within all social groups is based on the processes of exchange, cooperation, competition, and conflict;
8. that the only way to manage life in large, complex societies is through the establishment of formal organizations;
9. that formal organizations are administered through a system called a bureaucracy.

TOPICAL OUTLINE

I. THE SOCIAL SYSTEM: STRUCTURE AND ORGANIZATION
    A. Elements of Social Structure: Statuses and Roles
        1. Statuses: Ascribed and Achieved
        2. The Multiplicity of Statuses and Roles
            a. Roles: Real and Ideal
            b. Conflict, Strain, and Confusion in Roles
II. GROUPS
    A. Group Size
    B. Primary and Secondary Groups
    C. Additional Classification of Groups

III. SOCIETY
    A. Classification of Societies
        1. According to the Chief Mode of Subsistence
            a. The hunting and gathering society
            b. The pastoral, or herding society
            c. The horticultural society
            d. Fishing and maritime.
            e. Industrial society
        2. Classification According to Social Organization
            a. Gemeinschaft
            b. Gesellschaft
IV. SOCIAL INTERACTION AND SOCIAL PROCESSES
    A. Social Processes
        1. Exchange
        2. Cooperation
        3. Competition
        4. Conflict
V. FORMAL ORGANIZATIONS
    A. Formal Organizations and Institutions Distinguished
        1. Characteristics of Formal Organizations.
        2. Types of Formal Organizations
            a. Normative Organizations
            b. Coercive Organizations
            c. Utilitarian Organizations
    B. Voluntary Associations
    C. Involuntary Associations
VI. BUREAUCRACY
    A. Dynamic quality of Bureaucracy
    B. The Informal Side of Bureaucracy

A. CHAPTER OVERVIEW

Because human infants are born helpless and must depend on an adult for basic survival, the human way of life is above all a group way of life. Living in groups has forced people to create systems of behavior based on communication of individuals within a group. Communication between two or more persons by means of symbols (language) is the basis of interaction, and is called **symbolic interaction**.

Interaction, through repetition, acquires definite patterns which eventually become a system. Thus, it can be said that human life takes place within a social system. A **social system** is a model used by social scientists to illustrate how social relationships work in a society. The social system of any group has a **structure** and an **organization** that consist of the network of organized relationships among the individuals who make up the social system. A social system is not structured and organized into a fixed set of rules; rather, the processes that take place in it are dynamic, and stable and predictable patterns of behavior are continually redefined to fit conditions.

One way in which the social system functions is that individuals in a group have specific statuses and fulfill definite roles. A **status** is a **position** in a social group that implies **ranking** or value rating according to the values prevalent in the group. **Examples** of statuses are: mother, teacher, son, students, etc. What the individual holding the status **does** is his/her role. Status and role, then, are the two sides of the same coin. They come into existence because a group (society is a group) needs to have certain tasks performed for survival, and it is more efficient to have specific individuals perform specific tasks.

Individuals are **born** with some statuses--they are males or females, for instance; we say that these statuses and the roles attached to them are **ascribed**. Other statuses are **acquired**: we get married and become husband and wife; and we say such statuses are **achieved**.

Each individual has a **multiplicity** of statuses and fulfills a number of roles. The status most important to the individual and the group is called his/her **master status**. The large number of roles that people are called upon to play create **confusion** and **conflict** for some individuals; thus, faulty role performance is not infrequent, leading to mental illness, maladjustment, and general frustration.

A. FILL IN THE BLANKS:

1. Life in groups forces people to create a system of behavior based on communication.

2. Communication between two or more persons by means of language or gestures is called symbolic interaction.

3. A social system is a model that illustrates how social relationships work in society.

4. Repeated interaction gives rise to patterns of behavior which then are the base of the social systems.

41

5. Any social system has _structure_ and _organization_ .

6. The members of a social system have _statuses_ and fulfill _roles_ .

7. A position in a social group implying ranking and value rating is an _status_ .

8. There is no role without an _status_ because role is what the person holding the status _does_ .

9. Statuses with which individuals are born are called _ascribed_ .

10. Acquired statuses are called _achieved_ .

11. Individuals hold an _multiplicity_ of _statuses_ and fill many _roles_ .

12. The most important status an individual holds is called the _master_ status.

13. The large number of roles creates _role_ _confusion_ and _conflict_ .

B. CHAPTER OVERVIEW

In its sociological sense, the term "**group**" differs from an **aggregate**--which is a number of people who congregate in the same place at the same time--and **category**--which refers to a number of people who share the same characteristic. A group is composed of people among whom **symbolic interaction** takes place; there is recognition or **awareness** of group membership; there exists a degree of **consensus** about values, rules, and goals; and in which a **social structure** is evident, with members recognizing statuses, roles, obligations and privileges resulting from membership.

In most societies, there is an extraordinarily large number of groups. Therefore, classification is necessary. Some social scientists classify groups according to **size**: there are **dyads**, composed of two, and **triads** composed of three members. Small groups, such as families and friendship cliques, are the most important to the individual. Other classifications include those into "**in-group**"--people who are on our side, and "**out-group**"--all the others; **reference groups**, consisting of people whom we admire and whom we aspire to imitate; **voluntary** and **involuntary** membership groups--those we join for fun or profit, such as a runners' club, or those we are drafted into, such as the armed forces.

The most **important** classification, however, is into **primary** and **secondary** groups. A primary group is one that is relatively **small**, whose members are physically **close**, in which there is **intense interaction**, and which is fairly **stable** and of **long duration**. A **secondary** group tends to be **large**, and interaction within it is **short** and **businesslike**. Primary groups are very important to individuals: they represent their best support system. In modern societies, however, most interaction takes place in secondary groups.

B. FILL IN THE BLANKS:

1. An aggregate or a category of people is not the same as an _group_ of people.
2. To constitute a group, people must engage in _symbolic interaction_, be aware of _group_ _membership_, and have a consensus on _values_, _rules_, and _goals_.
3. One classification of groups is according to _size_.
4. Groups that are most important to the individual are: _dyads_, _triads_, _family & friendship group_.
5. Other classifications include:
in & out, _reference_, _voluntary_, and _involuntary_.
6. The most important classification is into _primary_ and _secondary_ groups.
7. A small group, in which there is intense interaction, which is fairly stable and durable, is an _primary_ group.
8. Short, businesslike interaction is typical of _secondary_ groups.
9. _Secondary_ groups are most common in modern industrial societies, but _primary_ groups are most important to the individual.

C. CHAPTER OVERVIEW

Society is the **largest** group of people inhabiting a specific territory and **sharing** a common **culture** and **social structure**. It consists of the **interrelated network of social relationships** that exist in the largest social system. Modern societies are generally nation-states, but in the past they were clans, or tribes, or large families.

Societies may be **classified** according to their **mode of subsistence** or according to their **social organization**. In the first kind of classification, historically there have been the following kinds of societies: hunting and gathering, pastoral, horticultural, agrarian, preindustrial, and industrial. **Industrial** societies are characterized by **urbanization**, massive **mechanization** and **automation**, complex **bureaucratization**, separation of institutional forms, and substitution of **impersonal** ties for kinship ties.

A more frequent classification is the one according to basic **patterns of social organization**. In this type of classification, societies are placed on the two extremes of an ideal continuum. At one extreme there is the **Gemeinschaft** society, also called traditional or communal, with the following characteristics: small size, little division of labor, the family as the focal unit of society, primary social relationships, patterns of behavior dictated by custom and tradition, homogeneity, with the society acting as an integrated social unit. At the other extreme there is the **Gesellschaft** society, also called the modern industrial or associational, with the opposite characteristics: large size, a complex system of division of labor, a large number of social institutions and occupational, political, and social groups. Relationships are of a **secondary** nature, patterns of behavior are regulated by formal and informal laws, the society is heterogeneous and multigroup, with diminished unity. There has been a visible **trend**, beginning with the late Middle Ages, for societies to shift **from** the **communal** toward the **associational** kind.

C. FILL IN THE BLANKS:

1. The largest group inhabiting a specific territory whose members share a common culture and social structure is _society_ .
2. Society is the largest _social_ _system_ .
3. Members of society are involved in an interrelated network of _social_ _relationships_.
4. Clans, tribes, and large families have been replaced by _nation_ _state_ in modern times.
5. Societies can be classified either according to their _social organization_ or their _mode_ of _substistence substistence_
6. Some of the societies classified according to their mode of subsistence include: _hunting & gathering_ , _pastoral_ _horticultural_ , _agrarian_ , _modern industrial_

44

7. Industrial societies are characterized by: _urbanization_, _mechanization_ and _bureaucratization_

8. A more common classification is into the basic patterns of
social organization.

9. Placed on an ideal continuum, the two opposite kinds of societies are _Gemein Schaft_ and _Gesellshaft_.

10. Some of the characteristics of communal societies are:
small size, _primary_ relationships, _little → of labor_,

11. The characteristics of modern industrial societies include: _larger size_, _social institution_, _complex_ division of labor.

D. CHAPTER OVERVIEW

Individuals in groups continually interact. **Interaction** is **symbolic** behavior, consisting of **words** or **gestures**. It is directed toward others and takes into consideration the reactions of others. Through repetition, interaction has acquired certain **patterns**. These patterns, called **social processes**, are said to be the chief elements of the social bond. The four **primary social processes** are **exchange, cooperation, competition, and conflict**. All other social processes are combinations of or derivations from the above.

Exchange is a transaction in which one of two individuals, groups, or societies does something for the other with the expectation of obtaining something in return of equal value. **Cooperation** involves two or more persons or groups working jointly in a common enterprise for a shared goal. **Competition** occurs when two or more individuals or groups try to take possession of the same scarce resource, tangible or intangible. **Conflict** is a hostile struggle between two or more individuals or groups for an object or value prized by each. These processes sometimes occur together, in the same interactive situation.

In a group setting, individuals must submit to some type of **order** or **control**. Society has been said to be the structure that imposes order on human experience. **Social control** is an outgrowth of social organization: it **results** when individuals **fulfill** the **roles** that go with their **statuses**. Thus, group life limits individual freedom in that if individuals do not fulfill their roles, tasks do not get done and chaos reigns. But freedom is of no use to the individual outside of a group.

45

D. FILL IN THE BLANKS:

1. Within groups, individuals are continually ___interacting___.
2. Interaction is of an ___symbolic___ nature.
3. Symbols consist of ___words___ and ___gestures___.
4. Repeated patterns of interaction are called ___social process___.
5. The three primary social processes are ___cooperation___, ___competition___, and ___conflict___.
6. Individuals must submit to a degree of ___order___ in a group setting.
7. ___society___ acts as the structure that imposes order on human experience.
8. Social control is the result of ___social organization___
9. Group life limits ___individual freedom___.
10. Individuals must fulfill their ___roles___ in order for social order to exist.

E. CHAPTER OVERVIEW

As societies become larger, more **complex**, and more heterogeneous, a **greater** extent of **organization** is necessary to channel, regulate, and direct those activities that in simple societies are directed by tradition and shared norms. One way of organizing activities efficiently is **through formal organizations**. Formal organizations are **groups** which exist for the **purpose** of achieving a **specific goal**. The **methods** by which formal organizations function--**bureaucracies**--are fixed so that they may be routinely repeated and performed by a number of different individuals. The **characteristics** of formal organizations are a **formal structure** in which systems and roles are fairly static and predetermined; **relative permanence**; a **hierarchical order** of authority; and a formal **program** in the activities and interrelationships of members, which are **systematic** and conform to abstract guidelines. Some formal organizations are joined by necessity; others, by **choice**. The latter are called **voluntary organizations**.

Large-scale formal organizations are administered according to the principles of bureaucracy. **Bureaucracy** is a **hierarchical system** for **coordinating** rationally the work of many individuals through division of labor and a chain of authority. Max **Weber**, an early

sociologist, determined that bureaucracy in its **pure** form--that is, the **ideal** form--should contain the following characteristics: specialization, a chain of command, a body of rules, impersonality, and selection based on merit and job
tenure. In Weber's view, bureaucratic organization is one in which specific goals can be attained rapidly and efficiently and with a minimum amount of conflict.

In reality, however, bureaucracies **do not work** as well as they should. Some problems: they become resistant to change; rules become rigid; the top layers of the hierarchy obstruct changes that are perceived as threats; they tend to initiate policies instead of implementing them; they try to perpetuate themselves, extending size and influence; members may forge alliances with special interest groups and/or politicians; mistakes can be attributed to the next lower rung of the hierarchy; and a kind of **immortality** develops, since few bureaucracies are ever terminated, yet new ones continually come into existence. At the same time, bureaucracies have a **dynamic** quality that enable them to respond to changing conditions in society, and they are sometimes **instrumental** in promoting innovation and translating the ideas of scientists into manufacturing and distributing products. Finally, although the bureaucracy of large organizations encourages attitudes of impersonality and formality, **informal networks** of personal relationships develop within this framework, sometimes defying the purposes of the formal organization, but in the long run **benefiting** it.

Formal organizations have a tendency toward **oligarchy**, which means that leadership eventually falls into the hands of a few persons. The "**iron law of oligarchy**" suggests that oligarchy is inevitable because rank-and-file members of groups are generally **apathetic** regarding the interests of the group, leaving leadership open to the few individuals willing to assume it.

F. FILL IN THE BLANKS:

1. While most activities in traditional societies are directed by tradition, in complex societies efficient organization is achieved through_____formal_____ _____organizations_____.
2. Formal organizations are _____groups_____existing for the specific purpose of _____achieving_____ _____a_____ _____goal_____.
3. The method of administration of formal organizations is called _____bureaucracy_____.

4. Formal organizations are characterized by _formal structure_ _____, _relative permanence_, _hierarchy of roles_, _a formal prog._ and an _formal_ _program_.

5. Bureaucracy is a system for administering _large - scale_ _formal organizations._

6. Bureaucracy is an _hierarchical_ system for coordinating _rationally_ the work of many individuals through division of _labor_ _____ and a chain of _authority_.

7. The "pure" bureaucracy should consist of: _specialization_ - _hierarchy_, a body of _rules_, _impersonality_, and selection based on _merit_ and _job tenure_.

8. Some problems of bureaucracies include: a resistance to _change_, rigidity of _rules_, attempt at increasing _size_ and _influence_.

9. Bureaucracies also contain elements of _dynamism_ that promotes change and innovation in society and _informality_ which works to the organizations' ultimate benefit.

10. According to the "iron law of oligarchy," the rank and file members of an organization are _unwilling_ to devote time and effort into it, so _a leadership_ is assumed by a few individuals.

TERMS TO REMEMBER

achieved status: A position attained through individual effort or merit.

aggregate: A number of people who are in the same place at the same time, but who do not interact with one another.

ascribed status: An inherited position--one that is not attained through individual effort or merit.

bureaucracy: The hierarchical system of administration prevailing within a formal organization. The hierarchy depends on job specialization, a set of rules and standards to promote uniformity, and an attitude of impersonal impartiality.

category: (Referring to people) A number of people who have some characteristics in common, but who do not interact with one another.

competition: A social process (form of interaction) that occurs when two or more individuals try to obtain possession of the same scarce object or intangible value using rules and limits.

conflict: A social process (interaction) consisting of a hostile struggle in which two or more persons engage for an object or value that each prizes, possibly to the point of destruction.

cooperation: A basic social process (interaction) involving two or more individuals or groups working jointly in a common enterprise for a shared goal.

dyad: The smallest type of group consisting of two members.

exchange: Exchange is the social process consisting of a transaction in which one of two individuals--or groups, or societies--does something for the other with the expectation of receiving something of equal value in return.

formal organizations: Large-scale associations of people in which most of the activities of complex societies are handled. They are highly organized groups displaying a formal structure, a body of officers, the expectation of permanence, and a hierarchical organization of authority (bureaucracy).

gemeinschaft: A small, homogeneous, communal, and traditional society. Relationships among members are personal, informal, and face-to-face, and behavior is dictated by tradition.

gesellschaft: A large, heterogeneous society, typified by the modern industrial state. Relationships among members tend to be impersonal, formal, contractual, functional, and specialized. Also called an associational society.

group: A number of people who engage in symbolic interaction; who are mutually aware of and influence one another; who recognize their membership in the group and are in turn recognized as members by the group; who are aware of the roles, duties, obligations, and privileges of membership; and who agree to a point about the behavioral guidelines, values, and goals they share.

in-group: Group to which the individual belongs and that confers on the individual a social identity.

out-group: Group to which others belong, excluding the individual defining group membership.

organization: A formal process that deliberately brings into existence a group of people to perform tasks directed at achieving a specific goal. It allows people who are unacquainted with each other to cooperate on complex projects effectively.

primary group: A relatively small group of people who live physically near one another and who interact intensely. Characteristics include stability, relatively long duration, informal and spontaneous interaction; and individual, personal, and total types of dealings.

reference group: A group providing individuals with standards against which to measure themselves.

role: The carrying out of a status. A way of behaving that befits a status and is transmittable as well as fairly predictable.

secondary group: A group that is in general larger and of shorter duration than a primary group. Interaction among members is formal, role-based, utilitarian, specialized, and temporary.

social organization: The network of patterned human behavior that is the product of interaction and that, at the same time, guides interaction.

social processes: Key patterns of interaction common to all human societies (cooperation, competition, and conflict).

social structure: The content of the social system, consisting of statuses, roles, groups, norms, and institutions.

social system: A conceptual model of social relationships in which each part is interdependent and interconnected to every other part.

society: The largest social group. An interrelated network of social relationships that exist within the boundaries of the largest social system.

status: A ranked position in a social group. Statuses are rated according to their importance in a social group.

symbolic interaction: Communication through speech, gestures, writing, or even music.

triad: A group consisting of three individuals. A more stable social unit than a dyad.

voluntary associations: Formal organizations that one joins by choice rather than out of necessity.

HOW MUCH DO YOU RECALL? TEST YOUR KNOWLEDGE

MULTIPLE CHOICE QUESTIONS

I.   A number of people who find themselves together in the same place at the same time are termed a(n):
a. social group
b. category
c. aggregate
d. collectivity

2.   Which item does not belong in a list of characteristics of a group?
a. symbolic interaction
b. reciprocal recognition of membership
c. structure
d. affection

3.   Which feature is needed for a collection of people to be considered a group?
a. face-to-face communication
b. personal friendship
c. mutual adjustment of behavior
d. awareness of common ancestry

4.   The most elementary social unit is called a(n):
a. couple
b. dyad
c. in-group
d. individual

5. Which is **not** a characteristic of primary groups?
   a. relatively large size
   b. physical nearness of members
   c. intense interaction among members
   d. stability and duration

6. Within secondary groups, interaction tends to be:
   a. of short duration
   b. specialized
   c. formal
   d. all of the above

7. The form of interaction that occurs when two or more individuals try to possess a scarce object or value is:
   a. conflict
   b. coercion
   c. contest
   d. competition

8. Social systems include:
   a. dyads
   b. organizations
   c. life-style enclaves
   d. all of the above

9. Which statement is **correct?**
   a. Statuses and roles are one and same thing
   b. A status is a position, a role is carrying out of the obligations of the status
   c. A status is what one does, a role is what one is
   d. only some individuals have statuses, but all fulfill roles

10. Which of the following statements is **false?**
    a. Each person occupies only one status and plays only one role in society
    b. Each person occupies many statuses and is expected to play many roles
    c. All statuses are not equally important
    d. We are evaluated and ranked according to our master status

11. Bureaucracy:
    a. has always characterized all kinds of societies
    b. is the hallmark of modern industrial societies
    c. is a form of organization characterizing large, complex, formal groups
    d. both b and c

12. Formal organizations that people join by choice are:
    a. institutions
    b. bureaucracies
    c. voluntary associations
    d. social groups

13. Horticultural and agrarian societies differ in that:
    a. agrarian societies involve the cultivation of grains
    b. horticultural societies create greater surpluses
    c. agrarian societies plow
    d. horticultural societies tend flocks and herds

14. Industrial societies are characterized by:
    a. urbanization, mechanization, and automation
    b. the substitution of primary relations for secondary ones
    c. the separation of institutional forms and the growth of complex bureaucracies
    d. all of the above

CHAPTER 5

BECOMING A PERSON : The Birth of Personality

In this chapter, you will learn

1.   that human infants must learn how to become human be-
     ings;
2.   that personality is based on a delicate interplay of heredity
     and environment;
3.   that the acquisition of personality occurs through the pro-
     cess of socialization;
4.   the various theories of socialization;
5.   who the agents of socialization are;
6.   that socialization occurs throughout a person's life;
7.   that one has to become resocialized to each new role in life;
8.   that socialization is not perfect and cannot totally overcome
     the existence of deviance.

TOPICAL OUTLINE

I. PERSONALITY
    A. Personality: A Social Product on a Biological Basis
    B. Heredity and Environment
II. BECOMING HUMAN: SOCIALIZATION
    A. Goals and Functions of Socialization
III. THEORIES OF SOCIALIZATION
    A. The Looking-Glass Self: Cooley
    B. The Self in Society: Mead
    C. The Self and the Unconscious: Freud
    D. The Transitional Self: Erikson
    E. Developmental Theories: Piaget
    F. Moral Development: Kohlberg
IV. AGENTS OF SOCIALIZATION
    A. The Family
    B. The School
    C. The Peer Group
    D. The Media
    E. Occupational Groups
    F. Reverse Socialization.
V. RESOCIALIZATION

VI. SOCIALIZATION THROUGH THE LIFE CYCLE
    A. Childhood
    B. Adolescence
    C. Adulthood
    D. Old Age
VII. PERSONALITY DISORDERS AND DEVIANCE
    A. Deviance
       1. The Relative Nature of Deviance
       2. Functions of Deviance
VIII. ATTEMPTS TO EXPLAIN DEVIANCE
    A. Biological Explanations
    B. Psychological Explanations
    C. Personality Disorders
    D. Deviance from A Sociological Perspective
       1. Social Integration and Anomie
       2. Cultural Transmission (|Differential Association)
IX. SOME CONCLUSIONS

A. CHAPTER OVERVIEW

Personality is a complex **system of behavior, thought, and emotions** that includes all of a person's attitudes, values, beliefs, habits, goals, and actions. It is **unique and dynamic**, in constant interaction with the external world throughout the individual's life. It is **circular**, affecting and being affected by the social structure. And it is **distinctive** because experiences exclusive to the individual are imposed upon a specific set of inherited traits and potentials.

Human infants cannot survive unless adults care for them until they reach a certain stage of maturity. Humans also have a strong **need** for social and **physical contact**, or love, remaining stunted or even dying when deprived ot it. Finally, humans **lack** strong **instincts** and must learn how to act to satisfy their basic needs and drives. All these biological reasons **predispose** human infants to **accept** the culture of the society into which they are born. In the process of learning what the cultural expectations are, **each individual** newly born into a society also **acquires a personality**. This is done through the learning process of **socialization** in which the social and cultural heritage of the group is transmitted to the new individual.

A. FILL IN THE BLANKS:

1. Personality is a complex system of ___behavior___, ___thought___, and ___emotions___.
2. Personality includes all of a person's ___attitudes___, ___values___, ___beliefs___, ___habits___, etc.
3. Other characteristics of personality are the fact that it is ___unique___ and ___dynamic___.
4. We say that personality is circular because it ___affects___ and is ___affected by___ society.
5. Exclusive experiences and inherited traits ensure that personality is ___distinctive___.
6. The biological reasons that predispose humans to accept culture are: need for ___care___, and for ___love___, and ___lack of instincts___.
7. Each newly born individual acquires a personality through the process of ___socialization___.
8. Socialization is the ___transmission___ of a society's social and cultural heritage.

B. CHAPTER OVERVIEW

Not only is **socialization defined** as the process in which society's cultural heritage is **transmitted**, but it is also that **process** by which a **biological organism** becomes a **human being**. The central point in socialization is that new individuals learn from the people around them. Other people are necessary for an infant to grow up to be human. An **isolated** individual, who has never known humans, can **never** become **human**, develop a personality, or be aware of self.

The **specific aims** of socialization are: teaching the fundamentals of life; instilling aspirations, transmitting important skills, teaching to fill social roles. A person's **identity** also develops in the process of socialization which occurs, ordinarily, in the context of the family.

B. FILL IN THE BLANKS:

1. A supplementary definition of socialization is that it transforms a ___biological organism___ into an ___human being___.

2. The central point of socialization is the need for *other* *people*.

3. Among the specific aims of socialization are: teaching *fundamentals*, transmitting *skills*, instiling *aims* and preparing for *roles*.

4. A person acquires his/her *identity* in the process of socialization.

C. CHAPTER OVERVIEW

Personality **acquisition** has been explained with **theories** ranging from detailed expositions of how socialization works, to the well-known **psychodynamic** theories of Sigmund Freud, as well as the more contemporary explanations of modern psychology. Sociologist Charles Horton **Cooley** theorized that the self is developed in response to either positive or negative reactions of others to the individual; thus, the self is like a **looking glass.** George Herbert **Mead** saw the development of personality in terms of **symbolic interactionism** in which the infant first recognizes symbols, then acquires language, replaces actions with ideas, is able to think of self as an object, and finally, through significant others and game playing, internalizes the cultural values of the society, developing a conscience.

The **psychodynamic** theories are based on the view that biological drives are of central importance to human behavior. The term psychodynamic is interpreted as meaning that the behavior of an individual is motivated by mental and emotional factors present within him. The most significant of the psychodynamic theories is the one set forth by Sigmund Freud which assumes the existence of **unconscious** processes that reveal themselves in **dreams** and in psychoanalysis. Freud insisted that an individual's **psychosexual development** occurs in stages, in the period from infancy to adolescence. The stages of psychosexual development are the oral, anal, phallic, latency, and genital. Each stage represents the individual's attempts to gratify the libido which is an instinctual drive toward pleasure that motivates human behavior. In the personality, the representative of the libido is the **id**, operating on a largely unconscious level; the **ego**, another part of the personality, functions on a conscious level forcing the id to satisfy its instinctual needs in a socially acceptable manner; and the **superego**, the third element of personality, exists to impose inhibition and morality on the id. The superego represents society and becomes an individual's conscience. Dysfunctions in the personality are caused by the disharmony among the id, the ego, and the superego that creates anxiety. In turn, anxiety leads to the development of **defense mechanisms**.

The **developmental** approach proposed by Jean **Piaget** holds that intellectual and moral development can only proceed in stages dependent on **physical maturation**. Developmentalists claim that people are active and capable of judging, interpreting, defining, and creating their own behavior provided they have reached a specific stage of maturation; they **stress free will and individual choice**.

Expanding on Piaget's ideas, the American Lawrence Kohlberg theorizes that children's **moral** development also proceeds in stages and develops from within the personality rather than being superimposed. Young children define right and wrong in terms of obedience and disobedeince to authority: their morality is **pre-conventional**. Adolescents adopt a morality based on socially approved values, trusting in a higher authority: they are at a **conventional** level of moral development. And some, but not all, adults reach a **postconventional** level that acknowledges the existence of conflicting values and attempts to resolve rationally any value conflicts.

The **family** is crucial to socialization because it is able to influence the individual in the earliest stages of development; because it meets both **physical** and **emotional** needs of the individual; because it is a constant influence in the individual's life; because it is **a primary group**; and because it determines the individual's status, at least initially. Other agents of socialization are the **school**, the **peer** group, **occupational** or recreation groups, and the **mass media**.

C. FILL IN THE BLANKS:

I. Personality acquisition has been explained by sociologists as occurring through ___Socialization___ and by psychologists through the _psychodynamic___ __theories_ of Freud and others.

59

2. Comparing socialization to a looking glass, _Charles Horton Cooley_ said that the self develops in response to the reactions of others to the individual.

3. George Herbert Mead saw personality development in terms of _symbolic_ _interaction_.

4. The psychodynamic theories of personality are based on the view that _biological drives_ are central to human behavior.

5. The most significant of the psychodynamic theories is the one proposed by _Sigmund_ _Freud_.

6. The intriguing notion of _unconscious processes_ that reveal themselves in _dream_ and _psychoanalysis_ is one of Freud's claims to fame.

7. Freud also maintained that psychosexual development proceeded in stages which are: _oral_, _anal_, _phallic_, _latency_, and _genital_.

8. Behaviorism contends that human behavior occurs through _learning_, and specifically through _conditioning_.

9. Developmentalism holds that moral and intellectual development proceeds through _stages_ dependent on _physical maturation_.

10. The _family_ is crucial in socialization.

11. Among the most important agents of socialization are: the _family_, the _school_, the _peer group_, and the _mass media_. _occupational group_

D. CHAPTER OVERVIEW

Personality development continues **throughout life**. Since people's **statuses** continually change, they must constantly learn new **roles**. **Profound changes**, in which entirely new sets of norms and values must be learned and old ones forgotten, are called **resocialization**. Prisons and long-term hospitals require the most extreme instances of resocialization. But resocialization also occurs at all stages of the **life cycle**, in childhood, adolescence, adulthood, and old age, as well as during periods of **crisis** in individuals' lives, as in divorce, the death of a spouse, the loss of a job, or the onset of disability.

D. FILL IN THE BLANK:

1. Personality development is a(n) _ongoing_ process because people continue to acquire new _statuses_ and thus are forced to fulfill new _roles_.
2. The process of _resocialization_ occurs when new sets of norms and values must be learned and the old ones forgotten.
3. In addition, resocialization occrs at all stages of the _life cycle_.
4. The most profound forms of resocialization occur in _total-institutions_.
5. Periods of crisis in a person's life also call for _____-_resocialization_

E. CHAPTER OVERVIEW

Life in society requires a sufficient degree of **order** to allow peaceful coexistence. By performing the roles that go with their statuses and by obeying most of the **norms** of the society, individuals ensure that the **social system** works. Norms and roles are learned through socialization, but the latter is never perfect; nor are informal controls adequate in large societies to maintain social order. **Deviance** refers to **behavior** that **conflicts** with **significant social norms** and expectations, and is judged **negatively** by a large number of people. Deviance is **relative** to time and place, to who commits the deviant act, and even to who does the defining. Deviance performs some **useful functions** in society: it strengthens nondeviants' faith in the value of conforming to social norms; it contributes to social stability; and it often heralds positive social change. On the other hand, **large-scale deviance** is damaging to the social order, and when it goes unpunished, it tends to **demoralize** those who conform to social norms.

Explanations as to why some people conform and others deviate from social norms have been offered by theorists from the perspectives of biology, psychology, and sociology. **Biological theories** attribute deviance to **genetically inherited** flaws. **Psychological** theories attribute it to **mental or physical disorders**, while **Freudians** blame it on the imperfect development of the **superego**. Personality disorders include **brain disorders** or mental retardation which are physical (organic) in origin but may become emotional disturbances. In addition, disorders may be **psychosomatic** (unrelated to a physical cause) or may consist of **neuroses** such as phobias, amnesia, obsessive-compulsive reaction, and dissociative reaction. The most **severe** forms of mental illness are **psychoses: schizophrenia, paranoia, and manic-depression.**

Sociological theories include the **anomie** theory (when there is a lack of balance in the social system and values are insecure, the individual responds with such deviance as **innovation, ritualism, retreatism, or rebellion**); the **differential association (cultural transmission)** theory (all behavior is learned in interaction with others in small, intimate primary groups); and **labeling theory** (that stresses the process by which individuals are labeled as deviant and their treatment as a result of that label).

Stressing an attempt at **improving** personality in order to derive more satisfaction from life, rather than being concerned with how personality develops, are Carl **Rogers'** and Abraham **Maslow's self-actualization** theories. Rogers maintains that a person must have unconditional positive regard from others in order to realize his/her self. Maslow suggests a hierarchy of needs that must be fulfilled if a person is to develop normally and develop his/her potential. **Gestalt** theorists stress the totality of behavior and individual perceptions of reality as they affect personality.

E. Fill In The Blanks:

1. The fact that some people commit horrible acts may be attributed to a failure of ___Socialization___, to the strength of ___temperament___, or to personality ___disorders___.

2. Departure from norms that is ___negatively___ ___perceived___ is the definition of deviance.

3. Since it varies according to circumstances, time and place, age and mental health, we say that deviance is ___relative___.

4. Deviants help define the bounds of ___permissible___ ___behavior___; hence, deviance has a certain ___function___ in society.

5. Deviance is conducive to ___social___ ___change___.

6. Impulsiveness and inability to defer gratification are traits that are ___genetically___ transmitted.

7. Psychologists assume that deviance is caused by ___mental___ ___defects___, ___illness___, or ___abnormalities___.

8. Colitis, ulcers, hypertension, anorexia, and asthma belong to the category of ___psychosomatic___ disorders.

9. Neuroses include _anxiety_ _reaction_,
phobias, _depression_, obsessive-compulsive reaction, hypochondria, and dissociative reaction.
10. _sociopaths_ engage in antisocial behavior without anxiety or remorse.
11. Psychoses include _Schizophrenia_, _paranoia_, and _manic-depression_.
12. Emile Durkheim introduced the concept of _Anomie/normlessness_
13. Conformity, innovation, ritualism, retreatism, and rebellion are part of _Robert Merton's_ theory of deviance.
14. A kind of _learning theory_ has been also termed the cultural transmission or differential association theory.
15. Primary and secondary deviance are elements of Howard Becker's _labeling_ theory of deviance.
16. Carl Rogers and Abraham Maslow are responsible for _self-actualization_ theories.
17. These theories stress the attempt to _improve_ personality in order to derive more satisfaction from life.

TERMS TO REMEMBER

anomie: Durkheim's term for a condition of normlessness. Merton used anomie to explain deviance, which he thought occurred when cultural goals cannot be achieved through legal institutional means.

cultural transmission (or differential association): Theory of deviance (Sutherland, Miller) based on the proposition that all human behavior, including deviant behavior, is learned through symbolic interaction, especially in primary groups.

deviance: Norm-violating behavior beyond the society's limits of tolerance.

differential association: See cultural transmission.

developmental theories: A school of thought in modern psychology whose chief exponent was Jean Piaget. Developmentalists hold that personality development proceeds in stages dependent on physical maturation (sensory-motor, preoperational, and concrete- and formal-operational).

ego: (Freud) A part of the personality that functions on a conscious level. It attempts to force the id to satisfy its instinctual needs in socially acceptable ways.

generalized other: (Mead) The individual's perception or awareness of social norms; learning to take the role of all others with whom one interacts, or of society as a whole.

id: (Freud) The representative of the libido in the personality, existing on an unconscious level and making up the primitive, irrational part of the personality.

instincts: Genetically-transmitted, universal, complex patterns of behavior.

labeling: A sociological theory of deviance that explains deviant behavior as a reaction to the group's expectations of someone who has once been decreed as deviant.

libido: (Freud) The instinctual drive toward pleasure that is the motivating energy behind human behavior.

looking-glass self: (Cooley) The process of personality formation in which an individual's self-image emerges as a result of perceiving the observed attitudes of others.

midlife crisis: What many people in middle adulthood experience when they reflect on their personal and occupational roles and find them wanting.

mind: (Mead) The abstract whole of a person's ideas.

paranoia: A psychosis characterized by the feeling of being persecuted or of being an important personage (delusions of grandeur).

personality: A complex and dynamic system that includes all of an individual's behavioral and emotional traits, attitudes, values, beliefs, habits, goals, and so on.

psychoanalytic theory: Theory of personality developed by Sigmund Freud. It assumes the existence of unconscious as well as conscious processes within each individual.

psychosexual stages: (Freud) The manner in which individuals attempt to gratify the force of the libido at different periods of physical maturation. The phases are oral, anal, phallic (or Oedipal), latent, and genital.

psychosis A serious mental disorder in which there is loss of contact with reality. Requires institutionalization when individuals become incapable

reinforcement: The use of rewards and punishments to achieve a desired behavior.

resocialization: A process in which the individual's existing self-concept and identity are erased in favor of a new personality more in keeping with the requirements of a total institution.

self: (Mead) The individual's self-conception or self-awareness.

significant others: (Mead) Important people in an individual's life whose roles are initially imitated.

socialization: The learning process by which a biological organism learns to become a human being, acquires a personality with self and identity, and absorbs the culture of its society.

superego: (Freud) A final element of personality, existing largely on an unconscious level and functioning to impose inhibition and morality on the id.

symbolic interactionism: A school of thought founded by George Herbert Mead whose theories center around the interrelationship of mind, self, and society, and include the belief that society and the individual give rise to each other through symbolic interaction.

total institution: An organization or a place of residence in which inmates live isolated from others, and where their freedom is restricted in the attempt to resocialize them with new identities and behavior patterns.

HOW MUCH DO YOU RECALL? TEST YOUR KNOWLEDGE

MULTIPLE CHOICE QUESTIONS

1.   The acquisition of personality occurs through:
      a. learning in school
      b. biology
      c. socialization
      d. maturation

2.   Socialization is:
      a. a process that ends in adulthood
      b. a two-way process involving the individual and others in interaction
      c. the process of erasing a person's existing self-concept
      d. a form of brainwashing

3.   The looking-glass self refers to:
      a. a theory of the emergence of the self
      b. the fact that we must look in the mirror to develop personality
      c. a theory developed by George Herbert Mead
      d. taking the role of others

4.   Personality is circular and distinctive because:
      a. it dictates how we see our roles
      b. our roles affect personality
      c. everyone has exclusive life experiences
      d. all of the above

5.   The family plays a crucial role in socialization because:
      a. it has the power to punish the child
      b. the child can only survive if its family takes care of it
      c. it influences the child at an early stage of development
      d. it has only a temporary influence in an individual's life

6.   According to Freud, an individual's psychosexual develop-ment occurs:
      a. in his or her infancy
      b. during adolescence
      c. in his or her maturity
      d. in five distinct stages from infancy to adolescence

7. The developmental approach to personality stresses that people:
    a. are basically passive
    b. can judge their own behavior provided they have reached a specific stage of physical maturation
    c. can be taught anything with the proper conditioning method
    d. never develop a full capacity for reasoning

8. Adults frequently undergo changes in personality as a result of:
    a. resocialization within total institutions
    b. occupational resocialization
    c. adversities in life experience
    d. all of the above

9. A self-indulgent playboy becomes a marine who is ready to die for his unit. We would call this change:
    a. reverse socialization
    b. resocialization
    c. secondary socialization
    d. remarkable socialization

10. Play is a critical element according to:
    a. Freud's psychoanalytic theory
    b. Mead's sybolic interactionist theory
    c. Merton's labeling theory
    d. Kohlberg's theory of moral development

11. Erikson maintains that identity crises:
    a. occur only during infancy through late adolescence
    b. can be successfully avoided
    c. occur less frequently after adolescence
    d. none of the above

12. Recent research by John Clausen:
    a. related success in high school to stable adulthood
    b. showed that some adults have very few crises
    c. concluded that most turning points in people's lives come before the middle years
    d. all of the above

67

13. Deviance is defined:
    a. in the same way everywhere
    b. in some cultures, as nonexistent
    c. in the context of time and place
    d. as another word for crime

14. According to Freud, deviance is caused by a(n):
    a. undeveloped Superego
    b. overdeveloped Superego
    c. unrestrained Id
    d. all of the above

15. An emotional disorder that allows one to work in society is called a(n):
    a. neurosis
    b. psychosis
    c. halitosis
    d. prognosis

16. Schizophrenia is:
    a. another name for split personality
    b. a term meaning "to hallucinate"
    c. applied to a number of disturbances for lack of any other label
    d. a psychosomatic disorder

17. Merton's use of the term "anomie" refers to deviance based on:
    a. lack of legitimate means to attain group goals
    b. mental retardation
    c. neurosis
    d. wild mood swings

18. According to cultural transmission theory, deviance:
    a. is learned in small, intimate groups
    b. is learned from books and magazines
    c. is learned from movies and TV
    d. transmitted in the culture

19.   Robert K. Merton views conformity as:
       a. an acceptance of cultural goals and rejection of the
       approved means of reaching them
       b. acceptance of both cultural goals and approved means
       c. habitual or compulsive pursuit of unacknowledged
       cultural goals
       d. rejection of both cultural goals and approved means of
       reaching them

20.   In the most correct sense, deviance refers to:
       a. any departure from social norms
       b. immoral behavior
       c. a departure from social norms that is perceived nega-
       tively by a majority of people
       d. any statistical rarity

21.   Gestalt psychology:
       a. stresses human self-actualization
       b. focuses on the individual's perception of reality
       c. studies biological drives
       d. eliminates specific problems through conditioning

CHAPTER 6

THE GREAT DIVIDE: RANKING AND STRATIFICATION

In this chapter, you will learn that

1. in spite of claims of equality, people are differentiated as to gender and age in all societies, and as to the amount of wealth, prestige, and power in societies that produce a surplus;
2. the importance of such differentiation lies in the social meanings that are attached to it;
3. ranking inherently results in inequality because it implies that some persons are or have more desirable attributes or things than others;
4. where scarce goods are distributed unequally, a stratified system results;
5. the theoretical explanations for inequality follow a conservative or liberal tradition;
6. social scientists have developed several models of stratification systems;
7. there is a variety of ways to determine social class;
8. the consequences of social class and the factors involved in social mobility affect human lives;
9. poverty seems to be an ineradicable kind of side effect of inequality.

TOPICAL OUTLINE

I. SOCIAL DIFFERENTIATION, RANKING, AND STRATIFICATION
  A. Stratification
    1. Theoretical Views on Stratification
      a. Structural-Functional Perspective
      b. Conflict Perspective
II. DIMENSIONS OF STRATIFICATION: CLASS, STATUS, AND POWER
  A. Class
    1. Definitions of Class: Marx and Weber
  B. Status
    1. Status Inconsistency
    2. Master Status

71

        C. Power
            1. Political power
            2. Social power
III. SYSTEMS OF STRATIFICATION
        A. The Closed Society: Caste
        B. The Estate System
        C. The Open Society: Class System
IV. DETERMINING SOCIAL CLASS
        A. Socioeconomic Status
V. SOCIAL CLASSES IN THE UNITED STATES
        A. The Upper Class
        B. The Middle Class
        C. The Working Class
        D. The Poor
            1. The Working Poor
            2. The Homeless
            3. The Underclass
        E. The "New Class"
        F. The "Overclass"
VI. SOCIAL CLASS AND ITS CONSEQUENCES
        A. Family Life
        B. Child Rearing
        C. Education
        D. Religion
        E. Politics
        F. Health
        G. Mental Health
        H. Arrest and Conviction
        I. Values
VII. SOCIAL MOBILITY
        A. The Upwardly Mobile: Who Are They?
        B. Social Mobility In the United States
VIII. THE RICH AND THE POOR

A. CHAPTER OVERVIEW

Social differentiation refers to the fact that all societies differentiate among their members according to criteria that are given social meanings (Example: to be thin is good, to be fat is bad). To differentiate is to give **more** of the **rewards** of society to **some** than to **others**. Differentiation usually occurs on the basis of **social class**, of **ethnic or racial** origin, of **gender**, and of **age**. Differentiation is possible because individuals are **not equal**: they

72

have different genetic traits, are born into different social classes, have different talents and degrees of intelligence, and have different socialization experiences. Although people are unequal and differentiated in all societies, in **complex** and affluent societies inequality and differentiation are **more evident**. The fact that inequality is recognized and differentiation accepted leads people to **rank** themselves from high to low. In effect, society is divided into layers, or **strata**: we say it is stratified. The most common type of ranking, called **social stratification**, revolves around the amount of **wealth**, **prestige**, and **power** each individual has. Stratification is a consequence of the way resources are distributed in a society, and is **present** in **every society** that has produced a surplus.

A. FILL IN THE BLANKS:

1. All societies differentiate among their members according to criteria with ___Social___ meanings.
2. The above means that the society decides what is desirable and what is not, and then _differentiates_ among people.
3. Differentiation usually occurs on the basis of _social_ _class_, _gender_, _race_ & _ethnicity_, and _age_.
4. People are not born equal because they have different _genetic traits_, _levels_ _of_ _intelligence, social_ _class_.
5. Inequality and differentiation are more evident in _complex_ and _affluent_ societies.
6. Inequality and differentiation lead people to _rank_ _themselves_ from high to low.
7. Social stratification is ranking according to the dimensions of ___wealth___, _prestige_, and ___power___.

B. CHAPTER OVERVIEW

Social scientists are generally of the opinion that some social inequality is **unavoidable**. Theories of social inequality are derived from opposing philosophical positions: conservative and liberal. The **conservative** position, which held that inequality was part of the **law of nature** and a product of selfishness and greed, gave rise to the **functionalist** school of thought. Functionalists stress the **needs** of the **society** before those of the individual and maintain that in order for the tasks of the society to be carried out efficiently, a **system of rewards** must be instituted to lure the most talented and hardworking individuals. Functionalists also empha-size the need for **order, stability, and balance** in a society and claim that a system of stratification has a stabilizing influence. (Functionalism is also called the **equilibrium** theory.) Embracing a more **liberal** view of human beings, conflict theorists maintain that the natural condition of society is **constant change** that results from **conflicts and dissension** in the society. Such change, even though disruptive, is often **creative** and of long-range **benefit** to the society. Stratification systems, in the conflict view, are **mecha-nisms of coercion** because those in positions of power impose them on the rest of society as such systems work to their advan-tage. The best known conflict theorist, **Karl Marx**, thought that all of history was a record of **class struggles** because of the unequal distribution of rewards in societies. Moreover, societies are strati-fied because one group tries to protect its economic interest at the expense of the other groups. In particular, the **private ownership** of the means of **production** led to the division of society into the present social classes. Stratification is a technique of **oppression** of one social class by another, but it can also lead to the eventual development of a classless society once the **proletariat** (the working class) realizes that its own self-interest lies in rebellion against the **bourgeoisie** (the owners of the means of production). The two theories are not mutually exclusive: societies exhibit both stability and consensus, and conflict and dissension.

B. FILL IN THE BLANKS:

1. Social scientists believe that inequality is _unavoidable_ .
2. The conservative tradition held that inequality was part of the _law_ of _nature_ and the result of human _selfishness_ and _greed_ .
3. Functionalists are modern descendants of the _liberal_ tradition.
4. Functionalists stress the needs of the _society_ over those of the _individual_ .
5. Functionalists also maintain that an _system_ of _rewards_ is necessary in order to lure the best people to perform tasks needed for the good of the society.
6. Conflict theorists believe that _conflict_ and _dissension_ are the natural conditions of societies.
7. According to conflict theorists, conflict is beneficial because it leads to _social_ _change_ .
8. The best-known conflict theorist was _Karl_ _Marx_ .

74

9. Marx thought that societies were stratified because _one class_ imposed the system on the others as it was in their best _interest_.
10. Marx thought that once the working class realized what was going on and rebelled, societies would become _classless_.

C. CHAPTER OVERVIEW

All stratification systems consist of **differentiation, ranking, institutionalization**, and the influence they have on individual personalities. In addition, they are all based on the **possession** of things that are scarce and therefore prized, things categorized as **class, status, and power**. People are assigned a rank in society according to these categories. **Social class** is an **aggregation** of people who stand in a **similar position** with respect to some form of **power, privilege, or prestige**. People belonging to any given social class display similarities in how they handle the experiences of life and in **life styles** sufficiently so that they become differentiated from others, and come to constitute a **separate level** (stratum). **Status** is the **ranked position** (high, middle, or low) of an individual **in relation** to other individuals within the social system. The rank is determined by how the role attached to the status is valued in the society. Status is very important to most people and affects almost all of our decisions.

In American society, social status is determined by **occupation, source of income, color, education, sex, age, religion, and ethnic origin**. The third, and possibly the most important, category of stratification is power. **Power** is the **ability** of one individual or group to **control** the actions of another individual or group, with or without the latter's consent. In short, power is the capacity to get other people to do what you want them to do. **Personal power** is the ability of individuals to direct their own lives; it is generally tied to wealth. **Social power** is the ability to make decisions affecting communities or the whole society. It can be held **legitimately** (as elected government officials) or illegitimately (as organized crime).

The concept of **life chances**, a term first used by Max Weber, helps to understand the importance of stratification to the individual. Life chances **refer** to the **opportunity** or **lack of it** that individuals have to fulfill their potential in society. Such opportunities are directly tied to the social class to which individuals belong: the higher the class, the more the opportunities, and vice versa.

C. FILL IN THE BLANKS:

1. Stratification systems are based on things that are _scarce_ and therefore _prized_ .
2. People are ranked in societies according to the categories of _class_ , _status_ , and _power_ .
3. Social class consists of a segment of people who stand in a similar position with respect to _power_ , _privilege_ , and _prestige_ .
4. Status is the _ranked_ position of one individual in relation to other individuals in an _social_ _system_ .
5. Status, in American society, depends on _occupation_ , _source of income_ , _color_ , _education_ , _sex_ , and _age_ .
6. Power is the ability of one individual or group to _control_ the actions of another individual or group with or without the latter's _consent_ .
7. People in full control of their own lives have _personal_ power; those able to affect communities or even the whole society have _social_ power.
8. Life chances refers to a person's ability or lack of ability to fulfill his/her _potential_ in society.
9. Life chances are directly related to the _stratification system_ .

D. CHAPTER OVERVIEW

The **class** system is a stratification system (others include **caste** and **estate** systems) that prevails in the so-called open societies. Theoretically, in an **open** society each member has equal access to material resources, power, and prestige. In reality, no existing society lives up to such an ideal, but the United States is one of the few that approximates it.

To determine one's social class, we use an index that measures socioeconomic status **(SES).** Although most Americans tend to assign themselves to the middle class, around 2 to 3 percent are actually upper class **(upper upper and lower upper).** The lower uppers tend to be self-made professionals and entertainment figures and represent the achievement of the American dream. The middle class includes almost one-half of Americans and is also subdivided into the **upper middle, middle middle,** and **lower**

middle. Although it is difficult to define, the middle class has become a **cultural symbol** in the society. The working class includes approximately one-third of the population and consists of people who work in **skilled, semiskilled, or unskilled blue-collar occupations** whose incomes generally fall below those of the middle classes. The working class is undergoing dramatic changes in the United States as a result of **globalization** and the shift of manufacturing to countries where labor is cheaper. But even in more stable times, this social class has always been subject to **layoffs and unemployment,** so that working people's financial situation has always been precarious. The Census Bureau listed 15.1 percent of Americans, representing approximately 37 million people, as living below the **poverty line in 1993**. Poverty in this society means a condition of having less income than the average person; we are not dealing with *absolute deprivation,* or not having enough income to provide the barest necessities for survival, but with *relative deprivation,* a condition in which people are deprived in comparison to others in their own society at a particular time and place. Poverty is chronic in families with a female householder in which no husband is present. The **working poor** are the percentage of Americans who work full time but earn less than the poverty level for a family of four. Additional social categories are made up of the **homeless,** the so-called **underclass,** the so-called **new class** and the **overclass,** categories that have originated in the past several decades because of the transition occurring in the economy.

Membership in a social class has consequences for the individual in all areas of life. Specifically, **life chances** vary greatly among the social classes, and there are striking differences in **child rearing, education, health, arrest and conviction rates, and values.**

D. FILL IN THE BLANKS

1. In an open society, every individual should have equal access to ___wealth___, ___power___, ___prestige___.
2. The class system is only one system of stratification; the others include ___caste___, ___estate___.
3. We can measure social class with the ___SES index___.
4. The upper upper and lower upper social classes represent approximately _2_ to _3_ percent of Americans.

5. Everyone's dream in the society is to become a member of the
~~lower~~ upper class because they represent the glamorous life.
6. The middle class encompasses almost one half of all Americans
and is divided into the _upper_, _middle_, and _lower_.
7. The working class is experiencing a great deal of discomfort as
a result of _globalization_, but it has always been subject
to _layoffs_ and _unemployment_.
8. About _15_ percent of Americans are described as living below
the _poverty_ _line_, which means that they have less income than the _average_ person.
9. Poor Americans are experiencing _relative_ deprivation rather
than _absolute_ deprivation.
10. Additional divisions into social categories include the working
poor, the _homeless_, the _underclass_, the _new_ class, and
the _overclass_.
11. The variation in life chances and lifestyles among the various
social classes and categories include such areas as _child
rearing_, _education_ health, arrest and conviction rates, and
values.

E. CHAPTER OVERVIEW

Social mobility in an open society is the individual's ability to
change social class membership by moving up or down the
ladder of the stratification system. In **vertical mobility**, the movement is up or down; in **horizontal mobility**, there is a change of
status without a change in class. The American dream, with its
stories of individuals who have risen from poverty to extreme
wealth, is an example of the **myths** that have arisen about social
mobility in the United States. Recent conclusions about social
mobility are: that Americans frequently **move both up and down**,
that there is more **downward** mobility than is at first apparent, but
that more people move into the top levels of the class system than
move out. Finally, **education** is a very important variable in upward mobility, and class origins are less important. Some upward
mobility, in addition, has occurred not because of **individual effort**,
but because of other factors: the increase in white-collar occupations, the low birthrate of upper-class people, allowing for an influx
from lower classes for some jobs, the arrival of unskilled workers
from rural areas and abroad forcing skilled workers into higher
status jobs. Special talents are often the key to spectacular upward mobility, but at the **two extremes** of the stratification system
mobility seems to be insignificant: at the top, there is an occasional

downward slide, and at the bottom the lack of education and inappropriate socialization work against upward mobility.

E. FILL IN THE BLANKS:

1. Social mobility is an individual's ability to _move up or down_ the stratification system.
2. In the United States, upward mobility is represented by the _American dream_
3. Research on mobility indicates that there is frequent _movement_ up and down, that more people move _down_ than it seems, but that more move _up_ than move _down_.
4. The most important variable in upward mobility is _education_
5. Upward mobility is sometimes spectacular as a result of _special talent_.
6. At the extremes of the stratification system mobility is _insignificant_

F. CHAPTER OVERVIEW

The most **tragic** result of inequality is the **existence of poverty** on a worldwide level. In democratic societies, large gaps in income which translate into gaps of status and power, represent an ethical dilemma.

The so-called **Third World,** which houses 77 percent of the world's 5.5 billion people and accounts for 60 percent of the planet's land area, faces **poverty** that is far more **severe** and more extensive than people in more fortunate areas of the world. In the Third World (consisting of societies that are primarily agrarian), it is the **majority** of the people who are poor, meaning that **hunger, unsafe housing, and disease** are their predominant everyday experiences. Even in First World societies, especially in the United States, inequality has **increased** in the past decades, with a minority becoming very wealthy, and the majority experiencing **stagnant** or **declining** incomes. This **reallocation** of income is accompanied by **technological innovations** affecting the entire society. The innovations have prompted a **transition** of the economy from a predominantly **industrial system** in which a multitude of products are manufactured, to a predominantly **information system** in which services are rendered, research is carried on, and information is passed on to consumers. The new economic system requires totally **different skills** that a large

79

majority of Americans has not yet acquired. There are indications
that the country is becoming **increasingly stratified** and divided.

F. FILL IN THE BLANKS:

1. The existence of poverty throughout the world is the most
dramatic result of _world poverty_.
2. The Third World contains __77__ percent of the world's _5.5_ billion people.
3. Poverty in the Third World means that the majority of people
suffer _hunger_, _housing_ housing, and _disease_ .
4 In the United States, _inequality_ has increased in the past
decade.
5. This _reallocation_ of income has been caused by
technological innovations .
6. Technological innovations are prompting an _transition_ from an
industrial to an _informational_ economy.
7. Because the new skills needed in an information economy
belong to only an _minority_ of people, the society appears to
be becoming more _stratified_ .

TERMS TO REMEMBER

authority: Social power exercised with the consent of others.
Parents, teachers, and the government represent different levels
of authority.

closed or caste stratification system: A system in which class,
status, and power are ascribed, mobility is highly restricted, and
the social system is rigid.

conflict theory of stratification: A theory of stratification according to which the natural conditions of society are constant change
and conflict resulting from class struggles. Inequality is the product
of such conflict, as one group is victorious over others and asserts
itself over the rest of society.

estate system of stratification: The prevailing system of feudal
Europe consisting of three estates of functional importance to the
society. The estates were hierarchically arranged and permitted a
limited amount of social mobility.

functionalist theory of stratification: A theory in which social inequality is viewed as inevitable because society must use rewards to ensure that essential tasks are performed. The natural conditions of society are thought to be order and stability (equilibrium).

life chances: The opportunity of each individual to fulfill his or her potential as a human being. Life chances differ according to social class.

open or class society: A society in which the stratification system allows for social mobility and in which a person's status is achieved rather than being ascribed on the basis of birth. Open systems are characteristic of industrial societies.

power: A dimension of stratification consisting of the ability of one person or group to control the actions of others with or without the latter's consent.

social class: A dimension of stratification consisting of an aggregate of persons in a society who stand in a similar position with regard to some form of power, privilege, or prestige.

social mobility: An individual's ability to change his or her social class membership by moving up (or down) the stratification system. Upward or downward mobility is vertical, whereas mobility that results in a change of status without a consequent change of class is horizontal.

social status: A dimension of stratification consisting of an individual's ranked position within the social system, the rank being determined mainly by the individual's occupational role.

social stratification (ranking): A process existing in all but the simplest societies whereby members rank one another and themselves hierarchically with respect to the amount of desirables (wealth, prestige, power) they possess.

stratification system: The overlapping manner in which members of society are ranked according to classes, status groups, and hierarchies of power. Analyzed on a continuum from closed to open.

structural mobility: Upward mobility caused by industrial and technological change that pushes skilled workers into higher status occupations.

HOW MUCH DO YOU RECALL? TEST YOUR KNOWLEDGE

MULTIPLE CHOICE QUESTIONS:

1.   Simple societies that do not produce a surplus may avoid:
   a. progress
   b. stratification
   c. conflict
   d. coercion

2.   Which forms of inequality are present in all human societ-ies? a. sex
   b. age
   c. wealth
   d. all of the above

3.   People tend to rank themselves in terms of the possession of:
   a. intelligence, beauty, strength
   b. wisdom, maturity, experience
   c. wealth, prestige, and power
   d. gender, age, hair color

4.   According to functionalism:
   a. society must reward the most talented individuals for performing necessary tasks
   b. garbage collection is as important a task as medicine for a society
   c. a system of stratification is undemocratic
   d. the natural condition of society is conflict

5.   Functionalist theorists:
   a. stress the needs of the individual
   b. stress the need for order, stability, and the importance of . society over the individual
   c. hold that all positions in society are equally important
   d. maintain that there is no need for a system of rewards

6. Which is **not** a statement of Karl Marx regarding stratification?
    a. All of history is a record of class struggles
    b. Private ownership of the means of production leads to a classless society
    c. In every society, one group protects its economic interest against the others
    d. The proletariat must rebel against the ruling class

7. ". . . an aggregate of persons in a society who stand in a similar position with respect to some form of power, privilege, or prestige" is a definition of:
    a. social class
    b. status
    c. power
    d. life chances

8. What is the definition of "status inconsistency"?
    a. The condition of people who are ranked higher in one variable of status than in another.
    b. The order of importance given to status variables.
    c. The mechanism used by high status persons to protect themselves from competition.
    d. A situation in which individuals lack both money and a good reputation.

9. Power is the most important dimension of stratification:
    a. only in complex, industrial societies
    b. only in hunting and gathering societies
    c. in all types of social systems
    d. in all agricultural societies

10. A person's position in the social class continuum affects his or her:
    a. life chances
    b. life styles
    c. child-rearing styles
    d. all of the above

11. Power:
    a. may be exercised legitimately or illegitimately
    b. affects the distribution of society's goods and services
    c. may affect individuals, communities, or societies
    d. all of the above

12. A class system:
    a. works best in market economies
    b. provides unlimited social mobility
    c. is based on inherited titles and landed gentry
    d. forbids inter-class marriage on religious grounds

13. Which of the following is an example of the estate system?
    a. classical India
    b. the current plantation system of the American South
    c. feudal Europe
    d. today's United States

14. America's affluent tend to be:
    a. more liberal than the less advantaged on all issues
    b. more liberal on many social issues
    c. more liberal on many economic issues
    d. no more liberal than the less advantaged on any issue

15. By the "New Class," Barbara Ehrenreich means:
    a. bureaucrats
    b. career politicians
    c. journalists, academics, writers, and media critics
    d. all of the above

16. While there is more upward mobility than downward mobility in the U.S.:
    a. most Americans experience little mobility
    b. real earnings have declined in some sectors of the economy
    c. it has become harder to climb out of poverty
    d. all of the above

CHAPTER 7

MINORITY STATUS: RACE, ETHNICITY, GENDER, AGE

In this chapter, you will learn

1. definitions of race, ethnicity, and minority;
2. how the majority has dealt with minorities in its midst;
3. the causes and effects of prejudice and discrimination;
4. some characteristics of the principal minorities in the United States;
5. that the United States is likely to become a different, multicultural society in the next century;
6. that people are also treated unequally on the basis of such ascribed characteristics as gender and age;
7. how we acquire gender roles;
8. why sexism is an ideology detrimental to both men and women;
9. that the United States is becoming a society with an increasing proportion of elderly people;
10. of the existence and meaning of ageism;
11. of the various theories used to study aging and the elderly.

TOPICAL OUTLINE

I. MAJORITY AND MINORITIES
    A. Defining Terms
    B. Common Characteristics of Minorities
    C. Bases of Minority Status: Ethnicity, Religion, and Race
        1. Ethnicity
        2. Religion
        3. Race
II. THE MAKING OF PLURALIST SOCIETY
    A. Ideologies Regarding the Treatment of Minorities
        1. Anglo-Conformity
        2. The Melting Pot
        3. Cultural Pluralism
III. MAJORITY AND MINORITIES: PROCESSES OF COEXISTENCE
    A. Segregation
    B. Accommodation
    C. Acculturation
    D. Assimilation
    E. Amalgamation
IV. IN THE WAY: OBSTACLES TO PLURALISM

A. Racism
B. Prejudice
    1. Why Are We Prejudiced?
C. Discrimination
VI. RACIAL MINORITIES
    A. Native Americans
    B. Asian-Americans
        1. Chinese
        2. Japanese
        3. Other Asians
    C. African-Americans
VII. ETHNIC AND RELIGIOUS MINORITIES
    A. White Ethnics
    B. Jewish Americans
    C. Hispanic Americans
    D. The New Face of America
VIII. WOMEN
    A. Biological Differences: Nature
    B. Cultural Differences: Nurture
    C. Sex Roles
    D. Gender-Role Socialization
    E. Sex Typing
    F. Agents of Socialization
IX. THE EFFECT OF WOMEN IN THE WORK FORCE
    A. The Women's Movement
    B. Changes in Sex Roles
X. THE AGING SOCIETY
    A. Sexism and Ageism
    B. Age Stratification
    C. Health
    D. Work and Retirement
    E. Finances
    F. Relationships with Others
    G. Widowshood
    H. Death and Dying

A. CHAPTER OVERVIEW

Social differentiation is not limited to the dimensions of stratification, gender, and age. Rather, it **includes** differentiation according to **race, ethnic background**, and **religion**. People belonging to groups that differ from the controlling group in society in race, ethnicity, and religion are called **minorities**. The term does not infer numerical inferiority; only the fact that as a category of people, minorities possess **imperfect access** to positions of equal **power, prestige, and privilege** in the society. Conversely, the dominant group, or majority, does possess access to high-status positions (although not all individuals reach them, of course); thus, its characteristics are considered desirable.

Because of wars or migrations, modern industrial societies tend to contain a number of minorities. **Racial minorities** differ **biologically,** so that differences are **visible.** **Ethnic** minorities differ **culturally** though they may be similar in appearance to the controlling group. **Religion** is often the cause for minority status. And **women**, although numerically superior, have at times been considered a minority because they have less access to power than men. The same is true of the **aged.**

Minorities have a **subordinate status** as a result of specific physical and cultural **traits** that the dominant group considers undesirable. They are aware of their differences and tend to stick together. They tend to marry within their group, at least for the first few generations, and minority status is inherited by descent.

At different times in our history, different ideologies expressed the feelings the majority had toward the ultimate fate of minorities in the society. The ideology with the greatest following originated from an attempt to superimpose white Anglo-Saxon Protestant (WASP) standards and values on all minorities. This ideology was termed **Anglo-conformity** and resulted in federal, state, and local **efforts** to **Americanize** immigrants by having them learn English, abandon their customs, become naturalized citizens, and finally by establishing immigration quotas that discriminated against immigrants from eastern and southern European countries.

The **melting pot** ideology developed during the l9th century when Americans began to believe that many immigrants could make important contributions to the United States. According to this ideology, it would be possible to **fuse** all the various stocks, both biologically and culturally, to obtain a "New American." The ideology proved unrealistic when it was discovered that **intermarriage** was occurring according to **religious** patterns--with a Protestant, Catholic, and Jewish pool being created.

Cultural pluralism is the ideology most **widely accepted** today. It stresses the desirability of each ethnic group **retaining** its cultural **distinctions** while giving its political and nationalistic loyalty to the United States. The ideal behind this ideology has not been completely attained, but it remains our goal.

Ideally, if all differences between minorities and the majority were to be eliminated, we would have an **amalgamated** society. In reality, minorities have reacted in a variety of ways to their status. Some have wanted to **retain** their previous cultural heritage while giving political loyalty to their new home and **coexisting** in harmony with the majority and other groups in the society; these minorities are **pluralistic**. Some have preferred to **absorb** the culture of the dominant group until they blended with it; these minorities are **assimilationist**. Some have given up their original language and traditions in favor of new ones; they have become **acculturated**.

The **majority** tries to maintain its high status by **establishing** and **enforcing** the **value system** and the **behavioral norms** for the society and considers deviant those norms and values which differ from its own. It also **obstructs assimilation** by institutionalizing its prejudices. Sometimes assimilation is forced; but generally **pluralism** is said to be the **goal**. There have been many instances, however, in which majority groups have expelled their minorities, or one minority, and resort to genocide (killing off an entire people) is unfortunately also familiar.

A. FILL IN THE BLANKS:

1. Additional ways of differentiating people is according to _race_, _ethnicity_, and _religion_ if these differ from those of the dominant group.

2. The term "minority" refers to a _category_ of people who possess unequal access to _power_, _prestige_, and _privilege_.

3. Modern industrial societies tend to contain numbers of _minorities_ because of _wars_ and _migrations_.

4. Members of racial minorities are visible because their differences are _biological_; ethnic minorities may look as the dominant group does, but their differences are _cultural_.

5. Among the characteristics of minorities are: awareness of _subordinate_ position, _sticking_ together, marriage _within the group_, status inherited by _descent_.

6. A number of different ideologies have been popular in the United States regarding the role of _minorities_ in the society.

7. The one that had the greatest following originally was the one termed _anglo-conformity_.

8. Anglo-conformity was based on attempting to have minorities become _Americanized_.

9. A more idealistic ideology, popular in the 19th century, was called the _melting pot ideology_.

10. According to the ideology popular in the l9th-century, it was possible to create a _New American_

11. To create a new American, it was necessary to _fuse_ both _biologically_ and _culturally_ the old stocks.

12. It was found that although the different immigratn groups did intermarry, they did so according to _religion_.

13. The ideology that allows for cultural distinctiveness in a national context is called _cultural pluralism_.

14. Minorities have coped with the majority in a variety of ways: through _pluralism_, _assimilation_, _acculturation_, _accomodation_ or migration.

15. Ideally, if a perfect blending would take place between majority and minorities, we would have an _amalgamated_ society.

16. In trying to maintain its majority status, the majority establishes and enforces its _value_ system and the _behavioral_ norms.

17. The majority also _institutionalizes_ its prejudices.

18. The ultimate method of dealing with minorities is through _genocide_.

B. CHAPTER OVERVIEW

The term **race** is subject to much **misinterpretation** (see Chapter 2). Scientists use the concept of race to describe **biological differences** occurring in the human species. People who share certain visible physical characteristics have been categorized into races. Unfortunately, in time customs and mental or moral characterics associated with members of specific races were thought to be a function of race rather than culture and thus capable of being transmitted through heredity. Thus the term race has become a **subjective, socially constructed** perception of reality, and not an objective term referring to the distinction between biologically different groupings of people. **Racism** is the **ideology** behind this mistaken use of the term, being the **incorrect belief** that both **physical traits** and general behavior are **inherited**. The implication is also that behavior is inferior or undesirable. **Racist thinking** is based on **stereotyping**, or extending common, uniform characteristics to an entire group, without allowing for individual differences, and as an ideology differs from ethnocentrism (see Chapter 3) that is simply a belief in the superiority of one's own group.

Racism as an ideology has **declined** in the United States, but hostile feelings against racial groups remain. Because of the unpleasant connotations of race, a new term, **ethnicity** has become more popular. Ethnicity **refers** to a group's **distinctiveness** based on **social and cultural** factors rather than on biological ones. Heterogeneous societies are made up of a number of ethnic subcultures.

Racial and ethnic groups are often hostile to one another. The most common evidence of conflict is the presence of **prejudice and discrimination**. Prejudice is making up one's mind about someone before examining all the evidence, and then refusing to change one's mind even if the facts do not support it. Prejudice is learned; it is thought to be encouraged by **insecurity, social isolation, frustration**, and the need to rationalize personal failure; it does not necessarily originate through contact; and it persists because it is emotionally satisfying. Prejudice may also be a psychological mechanism called **scapegoating**, which is a tendency of frustrated individuals to re-spond with aggression against a handy target; or **projection**, which is seeing traits in other groups that one secretly admires and wants to imitate but which are openly hated or feared.

While **prejudice** is an attitude or **feeling**, **discrimination** is **actions** taken as a result of prejudice. It is possible to have prejudice without deiscimination, and discrimination without prejudice, but as a rule the two **reinforce** each other. **Attitudinal** discrimination refers to a situation in which the rewards of society are **withheld** from target group members in spite of their qualifica-tions. **Institutional** discrimination refers to the system of inequalities built into the society apart from the prejudices of individual members.

B. FILL IN THE BLANKS:

1. In its scientific sense, race is a term used to describe _biological_ varia-tions in the human species.
2. People began to think that customs and behavior were capable of being _transmitted_ through heredity.
3. Racist thinking is based on _stereotyping_.
4. Stereotyping is attributing a common trait to an _entire_ group, without allowing for _individual_ differences.
5. Ethnicity refers to a group's _cultural_ _distinctiveness_
6. Conflict between ethnic and racial groups is evidenced by the presence of _prejudice_ and _discrimination_.
7. Prejudice is making up one's mind without _having all facts_ and refusing to change it in spite of evidence.
8. Discrimination is _acting_ on the basis of prejudice.
9. Prejudice is _learned_; it is encouraged by _insecurity_ and _social_ _isolation_ and it persists because it is _emotionally satisfying_.
10. Discrimination may be _attitudinal_, and _institutional_

90

C. CHAPTER OVERVIEW

Native Americans, the original natives of this country, have been decimated by wars waged by the settlers on them, and by the diseases brought by the Europeans. Economically, they are the **worst off of minorities**, having a large unemployment rate and one of the lowest average family income rates. Most live on reservations, chiefly in the Southwest, though enclaves exist in some urban centers and in rural areas throughout the country. Native Americans are intensely **tribal** and have been the least receptive to European culture. Some American Indian groups have learned successfully some capitalist business procedures, and are prospering.

Asian Americans consist of Chinese and Japanese, and of late, of refugees from the Vietnam conflagration. Chinese immigration began in the middle of the l9th century, mainly to California, where many came to find gold and ended by working to build the railroads. They were heavily discriminated against and their immigration was restricted; in spite of this, as a group they **have achieved** great **upward mobility**, through education and habits of hard work and thrift. The Japanese began arriving toward the beginning of the 20th century, also mainly to the West Coast, and experienced the same sort of discrimination, as they were described by prejudiced Americans to be part of the "yellow peril." They, too, however, held **values** that assisted their upward mobility: they were hardworking, frugal, and valued education for their children.

The present-day influx of Asians was caused by the problems created by Vietnam. **Asians** are the **fastest-growing** ethnic group and hold the highest median family income, in spite of lack of skills and education. In some localities, competition with natives has created problems so that the government has begun to restrict immigration on the part of persons wanting to come not because of political oppression, but simply in the search for a better life.

African Americans make up approximately l2 percent of the population of the United States, the **largest minority** group if one does not count women. Their immigration was involuntary, one reason for their status as a special minority group. Because their ties with Africa were totally destroyed, blacks had to **create a new culture** based on the experience of slavery in the midst of the dominant culture. It is generally agreed that slavery was responsible for the negative self-image of most blacks and for the consequent problems it has brought to the black family and the social structure of the group. The civil rights movement has done much to remedy that image, and legislation, such as the Affirmative Action Act, has attempted to remedy the slights done blacks by the denial of many opportunities. However, while many blacks have indeed risen in the stratification system, mostly as a result of increased amounts of education, a so-called underclass consisting of unskilled immigrants from rural areas remains stubbornly on the bottom.

White ethnics are the descendants of the Poles, Irish, Italians, Greeks, and other Slavs who did not resemble the immigrants from Great Britain and Germany, and thus were subject to greater amounts of **discrimination**. Some of these descendants have managed to rise socially, mainly through educational achievements that propelled them into the **professional** sphere. Others, however, remained in the ranks of the working class, living in urban enclaves in which they have retained a close-knit community. They tend to be resentful of the help they perceive the government as having given to the other minorities while they subsisted on their low-income jobs.

Among the **religious** minorities, Catholics and Jews were subject to prejudice and discrimination at the turn of the century and into the first several decades of this century. These feelings of hostility may have been directed toward their ethnic origin--eastern and southern European--as much as toward their religions. In any event, both groups have done **well** socioeconomically, being represented among the **highest earners** and in the ranks of professionals.

The **Spanish-speaking minorities** may be divided into Mexican-Americans, concentrated in Arizona, California and other western states, Puerto Ricans, concentrated in the cities of the eastern seaboard, and Cubans, concentrated in Florida, especially Miami. They do **not** constitute a **unified community**, nor do they have a common culture; but they do share a language and the Catholic religion. Mexican-Americans have a low socio-economic status, remaining in the ranks of unskilled and semi-skilled labor, chiefly because they remain **committed to Mexican culture**, retaining the language, and often returning to live after a few years of working in the United States. The Puerto Ricans have a similar problem: coming from an agricultural background, they can only offer **unskilled labor**, and most return to their native land after a few years. Both groups are becoming politically more committed to the United States, and their interests are consequently being better represented. The Cubans, who came following the revolution that brought Fidel Castro to power, are generally thriving because of their **middle-class professions** that fit in easily into a capitalistic system.

The **dilemma** facing the United States is **how** to achieve **pluralism** without **conflict**, how to live up to the motto "E pluribus unum"--out of many, one--that we display but have failed to live up to.

92

C. FILL IN THE BLANKS:

1. The largest minority group consists of ___blacks___ who have special problems because of having come here___inuduntarily___.
2. The negative self-image of blacks, as well as other problems, are attributed to the experience of ___slavery___ and the destruction of___cultural___ ___ties___ to their native land.
3. The most problematic segments of the black minority is the so-called ___underclass___.
4. The Spanish-speaking minorities are not a___community___but they share a common___language___and___religion___.
5. The low socioeconomic status of both Mexican Americans and Puerto Ricans is partly due to their lack of ___urban___ ___skills___, and partly because they lack ___commitment___to American culture.
6. American Indians, the original ___native___ ___Americans___, are intensely ___tribal___ and least ___receptive___to European culture.
7. Chinese immigrants arrived in the ___19th___century in search of___god___, and found employment building___railroads___.
8. Although considered part of the "___yellow peril___" the Japanese achieved upward mobility because of such values as ___hard___ ___work___, ___frugality___and ___education___for their children.
9. The fastest-growing ethnic group in the United States are ___Asians___ who are achieving great ___upward___ ___mobility___.
10. White ethnics are resentful of the help the government gives___other ethnic___groups.
11. The "American dilemma" remains how to make a nation of many into ___one___entity.

D. CHAPTER OVERVIEW

Even though we all born either men or women, we must become **socialized** into sex roles. Such socialization begins in the cradle: girl and boy babies are treated differently. By the age of 3 most children know what sex they are and how they are **expected to behave** (but homosexuals may not have gotten the message of society). Socialization into sex roles occurs through **conditioning, imitation** (identification with same-sexed parent), and **self-definition**, a part of the cognitive developmental model which holds that children perceive their environment, make sense of it, and place themselves in it. As to the **agents** of socialization, they are still the **family,** the **peer** group, the **school**, and the **mass media**.

Differences between men and women are of an **anatomical**, **genetic**, and **hormonal** nature. These differences certainly have effects on the behavior of men and women. But there are many **myths** about the differences: there is little evidence that females are more social, more suggestible, have lower self-esteem or are less achievement oriented, or that males have more analytic minds.

There is **evidence** that females are **superior** in **verbal** ability while **males excel** in **spatial** and **quantitative** abilities. Males, however, appear to be more **aggressive**, and females seem inclined to **nurture** infants and children. Whether the existing differences are the result of biology--hormonal--or of socialization experiences is still an **unresolved** question.

The fact that women have been **treated unequally** in most societies has had consequences on the lives of most women. Sex roles have been permeated by an **ideology--sexism**--that justifies the inequality between the sexes. The obvious effect of sexism is that many **options** have been **closed** to women who have been relegated for centuries to the roles of wives and mothers and little else. The women's movement and sociocultural change in the society has opened more avenues for women, but their roles still remain far from clearcut.

D. FILL IN THE BLANKS:

1. Socialization into sex roles begins in _infancy_.
2. Most children know what sex they are and how to behave accordingly by the age of _three_.
3. Socialization into sex roles occurs through _conditioning_, _imitation_, and _self-definition_
4. Differences between men and women are of an _anatomical_, _genetic_, and _hormonal_ nature.
5. There is evidence that females are superior in _verbal ability_ while males excel in _spatial_ and _quantitative_ abilities.
6. Males appear to be more _aggressive_ and females more _nurturant_.
7. Sexism is an ideology that justifies the _inequality_ between the sexes.
8. The effect of sexism has been that many _options_ have been closed to women.
9. The women's movement and _sociocultural change_ in society have opened some doors to women.
10. Women's roles may be said to be _unclear_ at present.

E. CHAPTER OVERVIEW

Although **aging** is a purely biological process, it has social consequences. We play **different roles** at different stages of the **life cycle**; each role requires **socialization**, carries with it privileges and responsibilities, and is valued differently by thesociety. **Childhood**, as a separate stage of life, is a **recent invention**: in pre-industrial societies, children were considered little adults and expected to fulfill adult roles. **Adolescence** is also a socially-invented stage at a time when there is a need for a better-educated and better-skilled work force.

Old age is the **final stage** in the human life cycle. In traditional societies, the aged have high status. But in industrial societies they do not because they are less knowledgeable than the young as a result of rapid advances in technology. The elderly must cope with **prejudice** and **discrimination** resulting from the ideology of **ageism** which attempts to justify the inequality in the treatment of the elderly by disseminating a number of stereotypes and half-truths. The most evident stereotype is that the elderly have such diminished mental and physical capabilities that they are no longer able to fulfill any productive roles. It is true that some elderly people do have diminished capabilities; but on the whole they are only a small minority, while a majority continue to flourish well into their seventies. Of course, **degenerative** disease **affects a proportion** of the elderly, and it is often made worse by worries about the high cost of health care which is not covered adequately by government insurance programs, and by feelings of depression stemming from loneliness and feelings of social isolation. **Mandatory retirement age**, whether it be 65 or 70, is another source of **frustration** as the ability to and desire to work are entirely individual matters and may force some to disengage before they are ready. **Disengagement** is supposed to be a mutual process by which the elderly give up social and occupational roles voluntarily so that these roles may be filled by younger persons. Other theoretical frameworks within which the elderly are studied include the **modernization, interactionist, subculture, activity, exchange, and age stratification** theories. As the population becomes older--the coming period in the United States has been termed "the graying of America"--our society must make better plans to accommodate this segment of the population.

E. FILL IN THE BLANKS:

1. Aging has_____social_____consequences although it is a__biological__ process.
2. The role of the elderly is not__highly____valued____in our society.

3. Childhood and adolescence are _socially invented_ stages of the of the life cycle that have been recognized only in industrial societies.

4. Rapid advances in technology make the elderly less _knowledgeable_ than their younger fellows.

5. The ideology of _ageism_ subjects the elderly to prejudice and discrimination.

6. One stereotype of the elderly is that they have _diminished_ capabilities to the point where they cannot fulfill _productive_ roles.

7. The main worries of the elderly concern the inadequacy of _health care_ insurance and _depression_ as a result of loneliness and social isolation.

TERMS TO REMEMBER

accommodation: A situation in which a minority is conscious of the norms and values of the majority, accepts and adapts to them, but chooses to retain its own, thus failing to participate in the host culture.

acculturation: The process of adopting the culture, including the language and customs, of the host country.

ageism: An ideology that asserts the superiority of the young over the old. Used to justify discrimination against the elderly in political, economic, and social areas.

amalgamation: The result of intermarriage between distinct racial, ethnic, and cultural groups, resulting in the erasure of differences between majority and minority groups.

androgyny: The possession in one personality of both male and female sex-typed traits and abilities.

anglo-conformity: The attitude, once held by the majority group, that the institutions, language, and cultural patterns of England should be maintained.

assimilation: A process in which a minority group is absorbed into, or becomes part of, the dominant group in a society.

attitudinal discrimination: Negative behavior against a particular group--or individual members of that group--prompted by personal prejudice.

cultural pluralism: An ideal condition in which the cultural distinctiveness of each ethnic, racial, and religious minority group would be maintained, while individual members would still owe allegiance to the society in general.

discrimination: Actions taken as a result of prejudicial feelings.

disengagement: A theory of aging which posits that the elderly withdraw from their former social and occupational roles so that these may be filled by the young. This should occur by mutual consent.

ethnic minority: A group that differs culturally from the dominant group.

ethnicity: A group's distinctive social, rather than biological, traits.

ethnocentrism: Belief in the superiority of one's own group.

gender: Psychological characteristics that develop when an individual is assigned to either the male or female sex. Expressed in terms of the adjectives "masculine" and "feminine" as opposed to genetically determined sex, which is expressed in terms of "male" and "female."

hormones: Chemical substances that, in the process of reproduction, are secreted by the glands of the fetus and thus determine the fetus' sex by stimulating or inhibiting certain chemical processes.

institutional discrimination: Negative behavior toward minority groups prompted by the knowledge that such prejudice exists on a societal level; that it is, in effect, a norm of the society. Includes structural form--found in structures such as government and the economy--and cultural form--in which the majority defines its own values, norms, attitudes, and interpretations of reality as the standards for the entire society.

melting pot theory: The belief that it is possible and desirable to fuse culturally and biologically all the various racial and ethnic groups in society.

minority group: Any group in society that is kept from attaining the rewards of society on the basis of culture, race, religion, sex or age. A category of people who possess imperfect access to positions of equal power and to the corollary dimensions of prestige and privilege in the society.

modernization theory: In the study of the elderly, the theory that the status of older people declines as the society in which they live becomes more modern and industrial.

prejudice: Prejudgment of an individual or group based on stereotypes and hearsay rather than on fact or evidence, and the inability or unwillingness to change that judgment even when confronted with evidence to the contrary.

race: An arbitrary manner of subdividing the species Homo Sapiens based on differences in the frequency with which some genes occur among populations.

racial minority: A group within a society that differs biologically from the dominant group in such features as skin color, hair texture, eye slant, and head shape and dimensions.

racism: The belief that racial groups display not only physical, but also behavioral differences, and that both are inherited and inferior or undesirable.
segregation: An attempt to isolate a minority from the majority.

secondary sex characteristics: Anatomical differences between men and women that develop when specific hormones are introduced into an organism.

sexism: An ideology that stresses that real or alleged differences between men and women point to the superiority of men. Used to justify inferior conditions of and discriminatory practices against women in most societies.

sex roles: The socially determined norms into which males and females are socialized and according to which they then feel and behave.

subculture theory: In the study of elderly, the theory that the elderly share a common set of experiences which makes them members of a subculture.

HOW MUCH DO YOU RECALL? TEST YOUR KNOWLEDGE

MULTIPLE CHOICE QUESTIONS

1. Membership in specific racial, ethnic, and religious groupings is:
   a. characteristic only of industrial societies
   b. a variable of the stratification system
   c. a biological rather than a social product
   d. the cross every individual must bear

2. The term "minority" may be defined as:
   a. a small group of people living within a large nation
   b. a group of people who possess the same access to prestige, privilege, and power but who differ in looks
   c. any group in society that is socially dominated by another group through discrimination because of race, culture, religion, sex, or age
   d. any small group in society which is disliked and abused

3. The difference between racial minorities and ethnic minorities is:
   a. in the size of each group
   b. ethnic minorities do not suffer from discrimination, but only from prejudice
   c. racial minorities are differentiated by physical appearance from the dominant group, ethnic minorities differ culturally from the dominant group
   d. racial minorities are smaller in number than ethnic minorities

4. Minorities have reacted to domination by developing goals that may be called:
   a. pluralistic
   b. assimilationist
   c. secessionist
   d. all of the above

5. Conflicts between the dominant group and minorities develop be cause:
   a. minorities are perceived as different
   b. minorities perceive themselves as different
   c. the dominant group has coercive power
   d. all of the above

6. Dominant groups tend to use all **but** one of the following methods in dealing with minorities:
   a. forced assimilation
   b. cultural relativity
   c. population transfers
   d. economic exploitation

7. Scientists agree that:
   a. there are three races
   b. there are fifty two races
   c. there are no races
   d. all of humankind is descended from the same common stock

8. Members of an ethnic group:
   a. share behavioral traits
   b. share social and cultural traits
   c. share physical traits
   d. are heterogeneous

9. The term "prejudice" implies:
   a. that one makes a judgment before having all the facts
   b. that one refuses to change one's mind even when confronted by facts
   c. that one takes action against members of minorities
   d. only a and b

10. Which is **not** a reason for the low economic and social status of MexicanAmericans?
    a. They are concentrated in agricultural and low-skill jobs.
    b. The nearness of Mexico leads to a retention of Spanish as the principal language.
    c. Parents tend to be ambitious and upwardly mobile which leads to rebelliousness in their children.
    d. The norms of their subculture do not encourage upward mobility.

11. The United States became a "triple melting pot" in that:
    a. racial, ethnic, and religious groups merged
    b. three racial groups emerged
    c. marriage among ethnic groups followed along the lines of the three main religions
    d. all of the above

100

12. The problems of Native Americans have been complicated by:
    a. tribalism
    b. lack of a common language
    c. the conditions on reservations
    d. all of the above

13. In Andrew Hacker's view:
    a. blacks have been given more than an equal opportunity
    b. being black remains the greatest stigma in this country
    c. blacks receive a disproportionate percentage of total personal income
    d. none of the above

14. William J. Wilson attributes the worsening conditions of the underclass to:
    a. a psychology of victimhood
    b. abandonment of the inner city by upwardly mobile blacks
    c. race-identifying protest leaders
    d. affirmative action and lowered educational standards

15. Latinos:
    a. possess a homogeneous common culture
    b. constitute a unified socio-political community
    c. are bound together by a common language and religion
    d. overwhelmingly oppose bilingual education

16. In the Puerto Rican community, "va y ven" means:
    a. the movement to the suburbs
    b. commuting back and forth to work
    c. returning to Puerto Rico after living in the U.S.
    d. none of the above

17. Concerning sex roles, it may be concluded that to a certain extent they differ because:
    a. men and women have different personalities
    b. women are nurturing because of their reproductive functions
    c. men are aggressive because they have to protect women
    d. males and females are treated and taught differently, thus developing different sex roles

18. Biological differences between men and women include:
    a. anatomical difference
    b. genetic differences
    c. hormonal differences
    d. all of the above

19. Which statement is **false**?
    a. All elderly are less productive than young people.
    b. Age differentiation is characteristic of industrial societies.
    c. A definite retirement age is a benefit the elderly have been working for.
    d. All of the above.

20. The most distinctive anatomical difference between men and women lies in:
    a. height
    b. weight
    c. reproductive systems
    d. hormones

21. Hormones are:
    a. toxic plants found in Latin America
    b. chemicals secreted into the bloodstream by glands located in the body
    c. found in food and drink with a wheat base
    d. man-made materials used in the making of perfume

22. It is through symbolic interaction that:
    a. individuals begin to label people and behavior as masculine or feminine
    b. people develop mental illness
    c. children decide to run away from home
    d. people learn how to make money

23. What is known as the "Women's Movement" had its beginning with the publication of:
    a. *The Scarlet Letter*
    b. *Gone with the Wind*
    c. *The Feminine Mystique*
    d. *God is a Black Woman*

24. Androgyny refers to:
    a. a movement of gay men and women
    b. the existence in one personality of both male and female traits
    c. being a transvestite
    d. fulfilling the roles of the opposite sex

25. The process that elderly people undergo when they willingly withdraw from many of their previous interactions and occupational roles is called:
    a. disengagement
    b. rejuvenation
    c. corruption
    d. self-denial

26. The process of growing old is known as:
    a. deterioration
    b. altercation
    c. senescence
    d. effervescence

27. Among humans, sex is:
    a. an instinct
    b. a drive
    c. an institution
    d. all of the above

28. Steven Golden's crosscultural research indicates:
    a. matriarchal societies occur as frequently as patriarchal ones
    b. patriarchy is a universal characteristic of societies
    c. women often dominate male-female relationships
    d. none of the above

29. Gender socialization takes place through:
    a. conditioning
    b. identification or modelling
    c. self definition
    d. all of the above

30. The double standard refers to:
    a. equal pay for equal work
    b. quota systems
    c. norms regarding the sexual conduct of males and females
    d. all of the above

31. Ageism asserts that:
    a. wisdom accompanies advancing age
    b. each stage of life has its own rewards
    c. the young are superior to the old
    d. life begins at forty

CHAPTER 8

CHANGE: THE EMERGENCE OF THE INFORMATION SOCIETY

In this chapter, you will learn

1.   that change is a constant feature of life, but the speed of change has become more rapid in the modern world;
2.   that change may be viewed from several perspectives: as modernization, as the consequence of war and conquest, or as the result of a world system;
3.   some of the sources of change;
4.   the processes of social and cultural change;
5.   some of the theories thought to produce change;
6.   the relationship of technology to change;
7.   the advent of the information society;
8.   the role the media play in the information society.

TOPICAL OUTLINE

I. SOCIETY AND CHANGE
    A. Levels of Change
II. PROCESSES OF SOCIAL AND CULTURAL CHANGE
    A. Social Change
        1. Planning
        2. Reform
        3. Revolution
    B. Cultural Change
        1. Innovation
        2. Discovery
        3. Diffusion
III. THE SOURCES OF CHANGE
    A. The Physical Environment
        1. Geography
        2. Population
    B. Ideas or Belief Systems
        1. Social Movements
        2. War and Conquest
    C. Random Events
IV. TECHNOLOGY
    A. Results of the First Technological Revolution
V. THE INDUSTRIAL REVOLUTION

A. CHAPTER OVERVIEW

Change is probably the most **dominant** element in the universe; thus, change in society is occurring imperceptibly all the time. However, although the condition of society may be constantly **dynamic**, it is necessary to freeze time in order to study society from the perspective of **statics**. But dynamics and statics are the two sides of the same coin.

The most obvious **causes** of change in society have been **technology**, **population** size, **urbanization, bureaucratization**, rising **expectations**, and the revolutions in **sex norms** and kinds of **weapons**. Technology has achieved a sophistication undreamed of by our ax-wielding ancestors, so that now machines perform not only physical but mental functions. Improved technology has always meant a **rise** in humans' **standard of living**, the **elimination** of many diseases, and a **prolongation of life**. This has led to increases in population which may finally be growing out of control. Modern technology, which is dependent on mechanization and automation, has brought about a **movement of people** toward **cities**, where the machines and the people who operate them can be housed in factories. **Increased production** necessitated a **better form of organization** on a large scale capable of coordinat-

106

ing the tasks of many individuals--a **bureaucracy**. Change has also been hastened by people's refusal to let things remain the way they are. The revolution of rising expectations is an attempt by third-world societies, and minorities within technological societies, to achieve the higher standard of living of the wealthier societies or groups. Technology has pushed women into the work force, and better methods of contraception have freed them from yearly pregnancies, all reasons for greater equality between the sexes. Finally, technology has created such effective weapons that we can destroy humanity with little difficulty.

A. FILL IN THE BLANKS:

1. The most dominant element in the universe is _change_.
2. We study society from the perspective of _statics_, though society is really _dynamic_.
3. One of the chief causes of change in society is _technology_.
4. Nowadays, machines perform not only _physical_ but also _mental_ functions.
5. Population size tends to increase as the _standard_ of _living_ increases, _diseases_ are eliminated, and _life_ is prolonged.
6. Technology has also led to _urbanization_ since machines and those who operate them are most efficiently housed in one place.
7. As business enterprises grew because of increased productivity, a better method of _organization_, called _bureaucracy_ emerged.
8. Third-world societies and minorities within technological societies have experienced a revolution of _rising_ _expectations_
9. Technology has freed women from frequent pregnancies and has pushed them into the work force, thus causing changes in _sexual standards_ and _attendant_ roles.
10. Currently the most hazardous effect of technology is the level of sophistication of _weapons_ that may lead us to destroy ourselves.

B. CHAPTER OUTLINE

Change in society results in **modernization**, an all-embracing process that involves primarily the change from a **preindustrial** to an **industrial** mode of production, but affects all areas of human life, not only the economic. The **technologically-advanced** nations are already modernized and are said to be entering a **postindus-trial** era. The less developed nations are trying to catch up as they see the high standard of living that industrialization has brought.

Modernization is not achieved without sacrifice. A totally **new system of production** is **superimposed** on a society that has survived at a subsistence level. In the process, many **traditions** and an entrenched way of life are **destroyed**. The social organization of societies is altered and a **new** type of **social organization** supersedes it. In Britain, for instance, farmers and serfs became industrial workers, moved to cities from farms, began to work in exchange for wages, accepted a secondary relationship with their employers, and started living in nuclear families. These **changes** resulted in **new values**, new **political** and **economic systems**, and even new personalities emerging. When **change** proceeds **slowly**, integration into the existing order, though difficult, eventually succeeds, and **accommodation** takes place. But when the change is **fast**, modernization brings with it **dislocations** and strains that evidence themselves in feelings of **rootlessness, anomie,** and sometimes **violence**. Such has been the case in the colonized nations that have been trying to modernize their economies as rapidly as possible, creating in this way conflicts with the established forces of tradition. The **political instability** in these newly-independent societies often results in **military dictatorships**, **millenarian religions**, **revolutionary** movements, and extreme **nationalism**.

B. FILL IN THE BLANKS:

1. Modernization is the consequence of___change_____.
2. Modernization involves primarily the change from a_preindustrial_ to an_industrial_mode of production, but affects_all__areas__-_of human life.
3. The technologically-advanced societies are entering a_postindustrial_ era.
4. With modernization, a totally new _system of production_ must be superimposed on a society that has survived at a_subsistence_ level.
5. The process of modernization destroys many_traditions_and an entrenched _way of life_.
6. In the example of Britain, people had to move to_cities__, become _industrial_workers, accept_wages_for their work,

enter into a _Secondary_ relationship with employers, and live in a _nuclear_ family.

7. Modernization results in new _values_, new economic and political _system_, and new _personalities_ emerging.

8. When change is slow, _integration_ into the existing order takes place.

9. When change is rapid, _dislocation_ and _strain_ result, leading to _rootlessness, anomie_, and even violence.

10. As a result, nations so affected are politically _unstable_.

C. CHAPTER OUTLINE

Technology includes all the methods, devices, and humanmade arti-facts that **help** people manage and **control their environments**. Some of the **technological** discoveries throughout history were so significant that we refer to them as "technological **revolutions**." Between 5000 and 3000 B. C. humans changed their condition from food gatherers to food producers by the invention of **agriculture**.

The agricultural revolution, which gave people a fairly **dependable food supply** (even a surplus), led to **population** growth; made people **settle** in one place; promoted the growth of **institutions** and solidified customs and traditions around the family, religion, government, and economy; promoted the establishment of **villages and towns**; instituted **division of labor** for greater efficiency; and encouraged trade between various localities. In short, people learned to control their environment better.

A new technological revolution occurred toward the **middle of the eighteenth century** when the invention of a small number of basic **machines**, the invention and discovery of some new **materials**, and the discovery of new sources of **power** combined to produce the **Industrial Revolution**.

The **effects** of the Industrial Revolution were the **mechanization** of agriculture and manufacturing, the application of power to manufacturing, the development of a **factory system**, a tremendous increase in the speed of **transportation and communication**, and dramatic **changes** in **economic** systems.

The Industrial Revolution is usually divided into three stages; it is thought that we arc still in the **second** phase, but are fast entering the computer age. **Computers** are responsible for a **knowledge explosion** that has doubled our ability to store and to have access to knowledge.

The Industrial Revolution brought in a **system of production**, or "industry," that was a **radical departure** from previous methods of manufacturing goods in that each task was divided into several steps that different people could perform. At first, merchants employed various members of a family to finish a product.

Eventually, they housed the workers and the machinery in the same place, called factory, where they had more control over them. Technology is also the practical application of knowledge; thus, it builds upon existing knowledge and technology. The more technologically advanced a society is, the more rapid is technological progress. **Modern industrial societies** are characterized by the **most rapid rates of change** ever known so that each generation's experience is unique. Technology has radically **altered human lives**; it is so important that some social thinkers believe that it determines society's culture (**technological determinism**). Moreover, it is thought that change occurs first in the **material culture**, and only later do values, ideas, and norms follow. Thus there is always a **culture lag** that produces **social problems** and disorganization (William Ogburn's cultural lag theory). However, change does not occur in isolation but in the context of a number of social phenomena; thus it has no **single** cause.

C. FILL IN THE BLANKS:

1. Technology includes all the __methods__, __devices__, and __artifacts__ that help people __control__ their environments.
2. The first technological revolution was the __agricultural__ revolution.
3. The stable food supply and surplus changed society in that it led to __population growth__, __permanent settlements__, and __institution-building__.
4. These changes led to the establishment of __cities__, division of __labor__, and __trade__.
5. A new technological revolution occurred around the __1750s__

110

with the combination of new machines, new _materials_ and
new _source of power_ .

6. Among the effects of the Industrial Revolution were the
mechanization of agriculture, the application of _power_ to
manufacturing, the development of a _factory_ system, and tremendous increases in the speed of _transportation_ and _communication_

7. We are still in the _second_ stage of the Industrial Revolution, but are fast entering the _computer_ age.

8. Industry was a radical departure from previous systems of
production , in that each task was _divided_ into several _steps_ .

9. In a factory, employers have more _control_ over workers.

10. According to the cultural lag theory, change occurs first in the
material culture, thus causing social _problems_
and _disorganization_ .

D. CHAPTER OUTLINE

Although the precise causes of social and cultural change can only be guessed at, the processes by which such change occurs have been observed. While change occurs contemporaneously on the societal and cultural level, for the sake of analysis the two may be separated. **Change in society** refers to change in the **patterns of interaction** when some individuals assume new statuses and fulfill new roles. **Social change** occurs through **planning, reform, or revolution**. Change in culture takes the form of change in norms, values, beliefs, and material objects produced by a society. Cultural change happens as a result of scientific discoveries, technological inventions, new achievements in the arts, shifts in religious doctrine, etc.

Planning is done by individuals in their personal lives and by governments at all levels. **Reform** involves efforts either by citizens or government agencies to correct laws or institutions. **Revolution** is change obtained through violent means when the government ceases to be responsive to the people.

The **processes** of cultural change are summarized as those of **innovation**, including discovery and invention, and **diffusion**. Innovations produce new elements or new combinations of old elements, and are always cumulative. A discovery is a new perception of an already existing fact or relationship. Invention is based on putting existing knowledge to new use. Diffusion is the spread of cultural traits from one society to another and from one group within society to another.

In addition to the above, change may also take place because of **alterations in the physical environment**--a volcanic eruption or repeated flooding that forces people to leave. **Shifts** in **population size** cause sociocultural change in a society. **Ideas**, or systems of belief, also cause such change. And finally sometimes single **individuals**, or **random events**, can have dramatic consequences leading to significant sociocultural change.

E. FILL IN THE BLANKS:

1. The precise causes of social and cultural change can only be _guessed_.

2. Change occurs _contemporaneously_ in the society and in the _culture_.

3. Change in society refers to the change in patterns of _interaction_ when individuals assume _new_ _statuses_ and fulfill new _roles_.

4. Change in the culture involves change in _values_, _norms_, _beliefs_ and _material_ _objects_.

5. Cultural change occurs through the processes of _innovation_, including _discovery_, _invention_, and _diffusion_.

6. Innovations produce new _elements_ or new combinations of _old_ _elements_ and are always _cumulative_.

7. Social change occurs through _planning_, _reform_, and _revolution_.

8. A discovery is a new _perception_ of an already existing fact or relationship.

9. An invention puts _existing_ knowledge to new _use_.

10. Additional sources of change may be found in alterations in the _physical_ _environment_, population _size_, or because of _special_ _individuals_ and random _events_.

F. CHAPTER OUTLINE

A number of social thinkers have concluded that the end product of social change, through modernization, is a **trend** toward **mass society**. A mass society is one that evidences a degree of **social disorganization** and is characterized by a **loosely** integrated social organization. A mass society need not be large in numbers,

but it is **composed** of **masses of people** who are widely distributed and **anonymous** in the sense that they may react to the same
stimuli, but have no reference to one another.

Mass society represents the **end** of the continuum from
Gemeinschaft to Gesellschaft societies (See Chapter 4). It is the
last stage in the transition from **primary to secondary** relationships. It is characterized by **high mobility, anonymity, specialization of roles** and statuses, and a **lack** in the ability of individuals to **integrate** themselves into the social system--more people
feel that they do not fit in. They make choices without regard to
customs, traditions, norms, and values.

The **danger** in a mass society is that the masses can easily be
mobilized and led by an **organized elite**. Masses engage in the
kind of behavior that social scientists call collective and that tends
to be unorganized, unstructured, and uncoordinated but also very
susceptible to action, including violent action, especially under the
direction of a charismatic leader. Western societies have **not yet**
reached the form of **mass societies**; only **tendencies** toward this
model are being reported.

F. FILL IN THE BLANKS:

1. The end product of sociocultural change, through modernization, is the trend toward a ___mass___ ___society___.
2. A mass society evidences a degree of ___social disorganization___
and is characterized by a loosely ___integrated___ social order.
3. A mass society is composed of masses of people who are
widely ___distributed___ and ___anonymous___.
4. Mass society represents the end of the ___continuum___ from
Gemeinschaft to ___Gesellschaft___.
5. Mass society is the last stage in the transition from ___primary___ to
___secondary___ relationships.
6. Mass society is characterized by ___high mobility___, ___anonymity___,
specialization of ___roles & statuses___, and lack of ___integrative___ ability.
7. The danger in a mass society is that masses can be easi-
ly ___led___ by an organized ___elite___.
8. Masses are subject to ___collective behavior___ that is unorganized and uncoordinated but also subject to ___violent___ action.
9. Western societies have not yet ___reached___ the model of the
mass society.

113

TERMS TO REMEMBER

alienation: A feeling of powerlessness and insecurity, of not belonging in society, producing boredom and meaninglessness. Alienation provides a fertile ground for social movements and is characteristic of people in mass society.

cultural change: Change in values, beliefs, and norms that may be brought about by scientific discoveries, technological inventions, new achievements in the arts, or shifts in religious doctrine.

cultural lag theory: The theory that different parts of a culture change at different rates of speed, creating dislocations and disorganization in the society. Associated with William Ogburn.

diffusion: A process of cultural change in which cultural traits are spread from one society to another (or from one group to another).

discovery: A process of cultural change in which an already existing fact or relationship is newly perceived.

invention: A process of cultural change in which old cultural ideas of existing objects are combined in new ways to produce ideas or objects more important than the previous ones had been separately.

mass communication: The relatively simultaneous exposure of large heterogeneous audiences to symbols transmitted by impersonal means from organized sources to whom audience members are anonymous.

mass society: The model (theoretical construct) of a society toward which postindustrial societies are drifting. It consists of an undifferentiated mass of people and an elite capable of dominating and manipulating it. It is highly urbanized and industrialized and displays secondary relationships, lack of traditional values, alienation, anomie, pressure to conform, and subjection to manipulation through the mass media.

modernization: Sociocultural change that transforms small preindustrial societies into large industrial ones.

social change: Change in the patterns of social interaction in which a substantial number of society's members assume new statuses and play new roles. Takes place through planning, reform, or revolution.

technology: All the methods and devices that help humans manage and control their environment.

HOW MUCH DO YOU REMEMBER? TEST YOUR KNOWLEDGE

MULTIPLE CHOICE QUESTIONS

1. Which is **not** one of the revolutionary changes that have transformed Western societies?
    a. The substitution of agrarian economies with industrial ones
    b. Dramatic increases in population
    c. The enduring role of religion
    d. Urbanization and bureaucratization

2. Which is **false** of social change?
    a. It occurs when some members of society assume new statuses and fill new roles
    b. It occurs through planning, reform, or revolution
    c. It must take place in material culture first
    d. All of the above

3. Cultural change:
    a. cannot exist separately and distinctly from social change
    b. occurs as a result of revolutionary changes of government
    c. refers to change in the patterns of interaction among individuals and groups
    d. is an invention of social scientists

4. Which is an example of cultural change?
    a. Fidel Castro's takeover in Cuba
    b. The Social Security Act
    c. The automobile
    d. Zoning laws changing residential patterns

5.   Which is an example of social change?
     a. The discovery of electricity
     b. The Cultural Revolution in China in which the roles of peasants and middle-class persons were somewhat reversed
     c. The use of steam to power machinery
     d. The sexual revolution

6.   When existing knowledge is put to new use it is termed:
     a. diffusion
     b. innovation
     c. invention
     d. discovery

7.   All the methods, devices, and human-made artifacts that help people manage and control their environment are called:
     a. automation
     b. technology
     c. instruments
     d. tools

8.   Which was **not** an effect of the Industrial Revolution?
     a. The mechanization of agriculture and manufacturing
     b. The application of power to manufacturing
     c. A reversal to older systems of economics
     d. The movement of people from rural areas to cities

9.   The production process became more efficient when:
     a. apprentices were hired instead of families
     b. machinery was installed in English cottages
     c. craftsmen began putting out their products for sale
     d. workers were housed in factories and a bureaucratic system emerged

10. Mass communication today is:
     a. public
     b. rapid
     c. outside of normal interaction
     d. all of the above

11. Change experienced on a middle level includes:
    a. the breakup of many nuclear families
    b. urbanization
    c. the incorporation of previously excluded groups within the political process
    d. the proliferation of career choices for individuals

12. Sociocultural change refers to:
    a. changes in norms, values, material objects
    b. reforms to laws and institutions
    c. the creation of new roles and statuses
    d. all of the above

13. The effects of war include:
    a. declining populations and labor shortages
    b. traumatic memories and forced contact with other cultures
    c. the growth of centralized government and war-related industries
    d. all of the above

14. According to Daniel Bell, the third technological revolution consists of the:
    a. joining of computers with telecommunications
    b. development of petrochemicals and synthetics
    c. applications of steam power to manufacturing
    d. advent of telephones

15. Third-world countries include:
    a. all communist nations
    b. industrialized, affluent nations like Germany
    c. less developed or developing nations, like Peru
    d. British Commonwealth nations, like Australia

CHAPTER 9

Population, Urbanization and Environment

In this chapter, you will learn

1.   the importance of the discipline of demography and its various concepts;
2.   the types of changes that occur within populations and their effects on societies;
3.   the dangers of overpopulation;
4.   the several theories of population;
5.   the meaning and effects of urbanization;
6.   the different nature of cities in preindustrial and industrial societies;
7.   about the characteristics of American cities;
8.   the difference between the process called urbanization and the attitude of urbanism, which has become predominant globally;
9.   about the emergence of suburbanization and metropolitanization;
10.   about the theoretical approaches to urbanization reflecting different views of the city;
11.   the nature of the urban crisis;
12.   about the discipline of ecology;
13.   the damaging effects of humans on the various ecosystems;
14.   the types of damage wrought upon the global ecosystem.

TOPICAL OUTLINE

I.   POPULATION DENSITY
    A. Demographic Processes: Dynamics of Population Change
        1. Birthrates
        2. Fertility rate
        3. Fecundity rate
        4. Death Rates
        5. Migration
        6. Immigration
        7. Internal Migration

II. CHARACTERISTICS AND COMPOSITION OF A POPULATION
    A. Sex Ratio
    B. Age Structure
    C. Tomorrow's America
III. POPULATION AROUND THE WORLD
    A. Malthus and Marx
IV. DEMOGRAPHIC TRANSITION
    A. Zero Population Growth
V. POPULATION POLICIES
VI. THE URBAN SOCIETY
VII. URBANIZATION
VIII. THE INDUSTRIAL REVOLUTION AND THE GROWTH OF CITIES
    A. Urbanism
    B. American Cities
IX. SUBURBIA
    A. The Impact of the Consumer Culture
X. METROPOLITANIZATION AND MEGALOPOLIS
XI. THE URBAN CRISIS
    A. Slums and Ghettos
    B. Population Drain
XII. ATTEMPTS TO RECLAIM THE CITY
    A. Urban Renewal
    B. The Future of Cities
XIII. THE NATURAL ENVIRONMENT
    A. The World We Live In
    B. The Ecosystem
        1. Overpopulation
        2. Environmental Pollution
        3. Environmental Depletion
    C. The Greenhouse Effect

A. CHAPTER OVERVIEW

One of the **side effects** of the Industrial Revolution that brought a higher standard of living to many societies has been the **growth of population.** Although overpopulation is said to be a problem that threatens future generations, it is differences in population **density** that are problematic -- some regions are totally uninhabited, while others average tens of thousands of people per square mile. The statistical study of such characteristics as birthrates, death rates, sex ratios, age groups, marriage and divorce incidence, and human mobility are studied by the discipline of **demography.**

There are a variety of ways to **measure** population density, which is a **relative concept**--what is considered dense for a farming area may be sparse for an urban area. Demographers have devised the categories of densely settled, moderately settled, thinly settled, and largely unpopulated.

Another **important** demographic **concept** is that of **birthrates** that are the number of births per 1000 people in one given year. **Fertility rates** are the annual number of births per l000 women of child-bearing age (15-44). **High birthrates** seem to occur in the **less industrialized and urbanized countries**, whereas highly industrialized and urbanized nations tend to have the lowest birth-rates. **Death, or mortality, rates** are the number of deaths per l000 people in a year. Death rates are **highest in tropical Africa and lowest in urban industrial nations.**

A. FILL IN THE BLANKS:

1. The growth of population has followed the improvement in the _____of_____resulting from the_____ _____.
2. Demography studies such subjects as_____, _____-_____, ____ _____,___ _____, _____incidence, and____ _____.
3. The crisis in population crisis is really the fact that_____ varies from very low to incredibly high.
4. Birthrates are the number of_____per_____women in any one_____.
5. The less industrialized and urbanized nations exhibit _____ birthrates, and vice versa.

B. CHAPTER OVERVIEW

The **population crisis** refers to the fact that the number of people in the world has been increasing geometrically (doubling) at ever shorter intervals of time. World population **doubles every 35 years**, so that every year there are about 75 million more births than deaths. Thomas **Malthus** predicted that this would happen and that the food supply would increase only in **arithmetic** pro-gression, so that eventually it would be exhausted, which would cause starvation. Great advances in technology, agriculture, and methods of birth control have tempered this prophecy, but it re-mains relevant in the developing nations. In the Western world, population growth was accompanied by an increase in the standard of living. In the past 200 years, the Western world has undergone a **demographic transition**, that is, from high mortality and fertility rates to **low mortality** and **fertility** rates. Demographers believe that this pattern will be repeated in other regions.

The United States has attained **zero population growth** as of 1972 (the fertility rates dropped below the replacement level). American women now have I.8 children; but this rate is likely to increase with changed circumstances. The human race is multiplying at a **very rapid rate**, and the most rapid expansion of population is occurring in **poor, underdeveloped nations**. Tensions produced by conditions in these nations may lead to conflicts on a world level.

B. FILL IN THE BLANKS

1. World population doubles every _____years.
2. Thomas Malthus predicted that food would grow in_____ progression.
3. The demographic transition has occurred in the_____ world where _____fertility and mortality rates have declined.
4. In 1972, the United States reached _____ _____ _____.

C. CHAPTER OVERVIEW

Although technology has provided effective means of birth control, lowering a population's birthrate is a **cultural**, and not only a technical matter. People have to become convinced that it is to their advantage to have smaller families, and they tend to do it in **urban environments** with industrial modes of production.

Food and population growth are highly related; on a world level, food production has grown faster than population of late. But **food production** is **not equally shared**. More than half of the food was consumed by the richest 30 percent of the world's people. Resources needed to support the Western lifestyle are **finite** and in danger of **depletion**; thus, it is prudent to plan to preserve them.

A final demographic concept is that of **age and sex distribution**, referring to the fact that populations vary not only in size but in age and sex, and that such inequalities have great **cultural** meanings for societies. A **graphic device** that indicates age distribution is the **population pyramid** that allows experts to predict population trends. In the United States the **median age** will continue to **increase** sharply over the next three decades; there are 6 million more females than males; whites have the highest median age; and the number of children under 5 has been shrinking.

C. FILL IN THE BLANKS

1. Lowering a nation's birthrate is a _____ as well as a _____ matter.
2. Populations vary not only in _____ but also in _____ and _____.
3. A _____ _____ allows experts to predict population trends.
4. In the United States, the _____ _____ will continue to increase sharply over the next _____ decades.

D. CHAPTER OVERVIEW

Urbanization is the **population trend** in which people **leave rural areas** to live in areas with a concentration of industry, business, and labor. The trend is the consequence of the fact that industry requires many workers, whereas mechanized agriculture requires fewer workers. Cities grew also as a result of **lower death rates, rising birth rates, and immigration**. The U.S. Bureau of the Census defines a city as an area with a population of at least 2500. Sociologists define the **ecological** city as an area composed of a **central city** with areas around it that are **economically and culturally** dependent on it. The movement of population in the United States has been from rural to urban to suburban areas. Only now is there evidence of a countertrend in that rural areas and small towns appear to be growing faster than cities.

Urbanization is an **ongoing** process. **Urbanism**, on the other hand, is a **condition** that includes a **set of attitudes**, and a quality of life distinct from the rural. Through mass communication, urbanism is being spread into all areas and is becoming a way of life for all. Consequently, it is destroying traditional rural values that revolved around primary relationships, historical continuity, and emotional involvement. These **traditional values** have been **idealized**: researchers found that small-town values are illusory, and that corruption and urban technology are rampant. Still, rural life is different from **urban life**. The latter is **characterized** by a **density** of physical structures, by the substitution of the **nuclear**

family for the extended family, by **secondary** relationships, by a **lack of group identity**, by a **freedom** from constraints because of anonymity, and by a resulting **increase** in **formal controls**--laws, codes, and regulations.

The transformation of American cities began with the trend toward **suburban** living. Suburbs now house more people than central cities, offering such advantages as more green spaces, larger homes, less pollution, and greater safety. Suburbs have themselves become commercial, industrial, and recreational centers to the point of being **economically self sufficient**. The suburban trend has removed an important tax base from cities, forcing them to curtail many services, with the result that additional suburban migration occurs. Such a movement has left the lower socioeconomic groups as the primary residents of inner cities. Because suburbs are so prevalent, the Bureau of the Census uses SMSAs (**Standard Metropolitan Statistical Areas**) to measure units of population. A SMSA is an **area** consisting of one or two **central cities, suburbs, and small satellite municipalities**. In locations where one SMSA is joined to another without interruption, the condition is called **urban sprawl**, or **megalopolis**, which has negative aspects in that it drains off resources of the city and creates conflicts among the large numbers of local governments.

The **urban crisis** has been intensified by the **move** of the middle class and industry to the **suburbs**. Inner cities overwhelmingly contain slums and/or ghettos from which the deprived and the trapped have little opportunity to leave. Cities, however, tend to have more **vitality** than suburbs because of the more varied group of people who inhabit them. Herbert **Gans** categorized urban dwellers as cosmopolites, the unmarried or childless, the ethnic villagers, the deprived, and the trapped. The first two categories are responsible for a trend toward **gentrification**, or an attempt to refurbish the decaying homes and neighborhoods. This trend may succeed where **urban renewal**, funded and administered by the government, has so far failed.

D. FILL IN THE BLANKS

1. _____ is the shift in population from rural to urban areas.
2. Central city degeneration and urban crisis result, at least partially, from the trend toward _____.

3. Additional reasons for the growth of cities are_____ ____
_____,_____ _____, and _____.
4. A city, as defined by the U. S. Bureau of the Census, has at
least_____inhabitants.
5. Urbanism is a_____that includes a set of_____
and a____ of_____distinct from the rural.
6. Urbanism is replacing traditional_____values that include _____ _____,_____ _____,
and_____ _____.
7. The most important trend, one that has created a crisis situation
for the cities, has been_____.
8. The U. S. Bureau of the Census measures population units in
terms of_____, and an uninterrupted string of them is called

_____.
9. Inner cities invariably contain_____and_____
which house those who have no _____to leave.
10. _____may succeed where _____
has failed.

E. CHAPTER OUTLINE

Populations are analyzed within the framework of their natural
environment. The **natural environment** is the total **complex** of
natural conditions and resources that **characterizes** a specific
area. It consists of elements such as **landforms**, **climate**, natural
vegetation, soils, native **animal life**, underground and surface
waters, and mineral **resources**. These elements change in time
and location.

There is a **reciprocal relationship** between the environment and
people and their cultures. The environment affects people's lives,
and in turn it is affected by them, often in a negative way. However, the relationship is not simple and direct. People can live
differently in similar environments, and differently at different times
in the same environment. The **same environment** is **perceived
differently** and **exploited** differently at different times in history, or
by different people.

High population density radically **alters** the environment. According to some experts, the environment is now in danger, its contin-
ued existence threatened for humans and other species as well. In
this case, too, the relationship is reciprocal as changes in the
environment can modify an area's population density (a damaged

environment forces people out of the area). Nonetheless, the **ecological crisis** is not caused by overpopulation or high density alone.

E. FILL IN THE BLANKS

1. The natural environment is the total complex of_____ _____ and _____that characterizes specific areas.
2. It consists of _____ _____, _____, _____, _____, _____, _____and_____.
3. There is a _____relationship between the natural environ-ment and _____and their cultures.
4. This relationship is not_____ and_____.
5. The same environment may be _____and_____dif-ferently at different times and by different people.
6. The environment is radically altered by _____

_____ _____.
7. Changes in environment also affect_____.
8. The ecological crisis is not caused by _____ or _____ _____alone.

F. CHAPTER OUTLINE

The technology spawned by the **Industrial Revolution**, in spite of the many benefits it brought humanity, is now **endangering hu-man life** on earth, according to some scientists. Part of the prob-lem is our notion that we are in control of the world and need not worry about what we do to our ecosystem. The **ecosystem** is the **way living things interact** and interrelate among each other and their environment. This interaction maintains a **balance** that permits life to continue. People, land, animals, vegetation, atmo-sphere, and social processes are so interdependent that slight alterations in one affect all others. Ecosystems may be **local** (a lake), **regional** (an ocean), and **global** (the planet Earth). The **harmony** of the various ecosystems has been disturbed by environmental **pollution**, environmental **depletion**, and **overpopulation**.

Pollution is the result of human tampering with the environment that has harmful consequences. **Pollutants** are sometimes unfore-seen and unwanted **byproducts** of human activities. **Air** pollution is caused by the **burning of fossil fuels** such as oil, natural gas, and coal. It has taken the form of **acid rain** and threats to the ozone layer. The first kills off some fish in lakes and rivers, and damages buildings; the second may result in a change of climate, the destruction of animal and plant life, a greater incidence of skin cancer and damage of a genetic nature, and reduced crop yields. **Water** pollution results from **oil spills** and dumping of wastes as well as from organic sewage, the overfertilization of water by excess nutrients, organic and inorganic chemicals, and sediments from soil erosion, radioactive substances, and waste heat from power plants. Herbicides, pesticides, chemical wastes, radioactive fallout, and garbage contribute to land pollution. Finally, prolonged exposure to intense noise damages hearing and increases irritability, preventing sleep, while certain forms of pollution lead to the deterioration of buildings, paintings, and statues, inhibits visibility, produces noxious odors, and obscures scenic views.

Even more acute than pollution is the problem of **depletion** of natural resources. No nation in the world is completely self-sufficient because once a natural resource has been used up, it is gone forever. The United States has to import a number of minerals already. Of most concern is the **depletion of oil** because our consumption of energy has been rising rapidly since the turn of the century. **Electrical power** is also undergoing constant increases in demand. Some experts maintain that nuclear sources are our only hope for the future, but others point to the severe limitations these sources have.

The Environmental Protection Agency has been established to deal with problems of pollution and resource depletion, and the Clean Air Act empowered the EPA to clean up the atmosphere. But pressures from the business community in weak economic times make rigid control difficult. Ultimately our **cultural values** will have to be changed in order to make any significant difference.

F. FILL IN THE BLANKS

1. The ecosystem is the way living things_____
and_____to each other and to the environment.
2. The interaction within the ecosystem maintains a_____that allows life to_____.
3. Ecosystems are divided into _____, _____, and
_____.
4. The harmony of the various ecosystems has been disturbed by_____ _____,_____ _____, and _____.

5. Pollution is the result of human_____with the environment that has_____results.
6. Air pollution is caused by the_____of _____ _____for
energy.
7. Acid rain and threats to the ozone layer are forms of_____
_____.
8. Oil spills and dumping of waste products are forms of
_____ _____.
9. Even more acute than pollution is the problem of_____
_____.
10. Rigid control by the_____is difficult because of pressures
from the_____ _____, especially in a weak economy.

TERMS TO REMEMBER

biosphere: A thin film of air, water, and soil surrounding the earth.

birthrates: The number of births per 1000 persons in a specific
population per year.

death rates: The number of deaths per 1000 persons in a specific
population per year. Same as mortality rate.

demography: The study of the growth or decline of populations,
their distribution throughout the world, and their composition.

ecology: The study of the relationship between living organisms
and their environments.

ecosystem: The way living and nonliving entities interact and
maintain a balance that permits life to continue.

fecundity: The biological potential for producing offspring.

fertility: The number of actual births per 1000 women between the
ages of 15 and 44.

infant mortality: The rate that reflects the number of deaths
among infants under one year of age for every 1000 live births.

life expectancy: The average number of years that a person at a given age can expect to live.

megalopolis: A complex in which one metropolitan area follows another without interruption. Also called urban sprawl.

metropolitanization: The tendency of suburbs, small cities, and surrounding rural areas to cluster around a central city and be considered as a single unit.

mortality rates: The number of deaths in a population per year.

pollution: The degradation of air, land, and water as well as the esthetic aspects of the environment.

population density: The ratio of people to a land area.

population pyramid: A graphic expression of the age and sex distribution of a given population.

sex ratio: Ratio of the number of males in a population in any single year per 100 females.

suburbs: Smaller communities on the outskirts of central cities and somewhat dependent on them.

standard metropolitan statistical area (SMSA): Term used by the United States Bureau of the Census to designate units of population consisting of a county or counties that include a city of 50,000 or more people.

urbanism: A condition, a set of attitudes, a quality, or a way of life distinct from the rural.

urbanization: A population trend in which cities grow at the expense of rural areas.

zero population growth: A condition in which each person replaces himself or herself only (replacement level of 2.1); thus, the birthrate and the death rate are the same.

HOW MUCH DO YOU RECALL? TEST YOUR KNOWLEDGE

MULTIPLE CHOICE QUESTIONS:

1.   Overpopulation is a problem worldwide but only in relation
        to:
        a. demography
        b. poor contraception
        c. population density
        d. political organization

2.   Population began to increase steadily:
        a. by around the middle of the 17th century
        b. with improvements in agriculture, technology, and
        medicine
        c. in the Bronze Age
        d. both a and b

3.   The number of births in a population in relation to every l000
        women of childbearing age is called the:
        a. fecundity rate
        b. fertility rate
        c. population pyramid
        d. population growth rate

4.   Which is typical of the first stage of the demographic transi
        tion?
        a. high birthrates and high death rates
        b. high birthrates and declining death rates
        c. declining birthrates and high death rates
        d. cycles of growth and decline

5.   Which subject is not studied by demography?
        a. birthrates, death rates, sex rates
        b. age groups, marriage incidence, divorce frequency
        c. human mobility
        d. rock-forming, land-shaping, soil-forming

6. Zero population growth:
   a. means that no more children are born
   b. indicates that the fertility rate has dropped below the replacement level
   c. must be achieved by all nations by the year 2000
   d. is actively pursued by the underdeveloped nations.

7. Demographers believe that:
   a. the demographic transition represents a general pattern
   b. Western societies are doomed to extinction
   c. the underdeveloped nations must increase their birthrate
   d. population grows in inverse proportion to food production

8. It is true of the population of the United States that:
   a. it is getting older
   b. there are more women than men
   c. rural and sunbelt areas attract the young
   d. only a and b

9. Birthrates:
   a. generally correspond to population density
   b. are low in western Europe and Japan
   c. are high in Arabia and Interior Africa
   d. only b and c

10. Most population experts:
    a. expect the growth rate to remain constant
    b. expect population to level off at between 8 and 15 billion people
    c. have written off the Malthusian prophecy altogether
    d. believe that a high fertility rate continues to be necessary in the developing nations

11. Urban families everywhere in the world:
    a. follow the dictates of religion and culture
    b. voluntarily curb their fertility
    c. have attained zero population growth
    d. willingly accept governmental family planning

12. Environmental pollution is the result of:
    a. dysfunctions in the earth's atmosphere
    b. ignorance on the part of the underdeveloped nations
    c. human actions that have harmful consequences
    d. unknown bacteria and viruses

13. The infant mortality rate in the United States:
    a. is the lowest in the world
    b. varies according to social class
    c. has no impact upon life expectancy
    d. is over 30

14. The United States became a bi-coastal society:
    a. when over 60 percent of the population lived on the east and west coasts
    b. because immigrants tend to settle near the port of entry
    c. because the rise of an information society sparked an internal migration to the coasts
    d. because federal policies have favored coastal states

15. In Third-World countries, the sex ratio reflects:
    a. higher birthrates for girls than boys
    b. female infanticide and general neglect of female children
    c. females' greater susceptibility to disease
    d. higher rates of conception for girls

16. One of the perceived advantages of suburban living is:
    a. concentration of apartments
    b. large variety of cultural resources
    c. older, more gracious housing
    d. greater safety from crime

17. Factors in the urban crisis include:
    a. the move of the middle class and industry to the suburbs
    b. the inner city's declining tax base
    c. a high percentage of deprived and trapped individuals
    d. all of the above

18. Urbanism is defined as:
    a. the migration of people from rural to urban centers
    b. a set of attitudes and a way of life distinct from the rural
    c. the growth of cities and suburbs at the expense of rural areas
    d. the study of the growth and decline of populations

19. The urban crisis:
    a. is intensified by the move of the middle class to the suburbs
    b. has been reduced by urban renewal
    c. has been intensified by gentrification
    d. is well on the way to being resolved

20. Ghettos:
    a. have similar conditions and problems to slums
    b. are formed in part through residential segregation
    c. tend to contain a particular ethnic or racial group
    d. all of the above

21. A megalopolis is:
    a. a few small cities clustered around a central city
    b. two or more metropolitan areas joined without interruption
    c. a suburb which has become independent of the central city
    d. all of the above

22. Urban ecology concerns:
    a. the creation of green spaces in urban areas
    b. the location and patterned growth of urban areas
    c. rebuilding central cities
    d. elimination of urban pollution

23. The essence of the consumer culture is:
    a. suburbanization
    b. the class system
    c. the focus on the acquisition of material things
    d. early retirement

24. Subcultural theory:
   a. explains why community declines with urbanization
   b. argues that cities are mosaics of urban villages
   c. explains why cities promote feelings of alienation
   d. none of the above

CHAPTER 10

COLLECTIVE BEHAVIOR AND SOCIAL MOVEMENTS

In this chapter, you will learn

1.   the meaning of collective behavior, and where and why it occurs;
2.   the definition and kinds of crowds, panics, mobs, riots, and mass hysteria;
3.   the definition of such collective behavior as appears in ru mors, fashions, fads, and crazes;
4.   the nature of publics and public opinion;
5.   of the collective behavior called social movements;
6.   of the traits and characteristics of social movements;
7.   about the theories proposed to explain social movements.

TOPICAL OUTLINE

I. COLLECTIVE BEHAVIOR
   A. Crowds
      1. casual
      2. organized
      3. expressive
      4. acting
   B. Mobs and Riots
      1. Rumors
      2. Fashions, Fads, and Crazes
      3. Panics and Mass Hysteria
II. THEORIES OF COLLECTIVE BEHAVIOR
      A. Contagion
      B. Convergence
      C. Emergent Norm Theory
III. PUBLICS AND PUBLIC OPINION
   A. Public Opinion
      1. The Formation of Public Opinion
      2. The Mass Media
   B. Measuring Public Opinion
      1. Sampling
      2. Interpretation
   C. Propaganda and Censorship

IV. SOCIAL MOVEMENTS
    A. Types of Social Movements
        1. Alternative
        2. Redemptive
        3. Expressive
        4. Reform
        5. Revolutionary
            a. nationalistic
            b. class
        6. Change-resistant
    B. Stages in Social Movements
        1. Emergence
        2. Coalescence
        3. Bureaucratization
        4. Decline
    C. Conditions for the Rise of Social Movements
        1. relative deprivation
        2. failure of rising expectations
    D. Theories Explaining the Rise of Social Movements
        1. Mass Society
        2. Structural Strain
       3. Resource Mobilization

A. CHAPTER OVERVIEW

Collective behavior is behavior that takes place without clear-cut **direction** from the normative system of culture; it is rather un-planned, and its effects unforeseen. It is **spontaneous, unstructured behavior** (or ways of thinking or feeling) engaged in by large numbers of people. There is never a complete lack of structure in the behavior of any group of people, so that collective behavior is really partly structured and partly unstructured. This type of behavior is frequent in periods of **rapid social change**, when cultural norms are in transition or are poorly defined. In turn, collective behavior may **trigger** sociocultural **change** and the adoption of new values.

Collective behavior occurs most often in **crowd** situations. A crowd is a temporary collection of people who respond to the same stimulus. There are **casual** crowds (people waiting at a red light), **organized** crowds (a concert or football game), **expressive** crowds (a protest rally or religious revival meeting), and **acting** crowds (mob, riots, violent protest meetings). Any crowd can become a

panic crowd, a **mob**, or a **riot** if the right stimuli are present, but an organized crowd is particularly receptive to mob behavior.

People in crowds tend to develop a **common mood**; ideas of what constitutes acceptable behavior emerge at the moment, and the behavior may be of an antisocial nature. A crowd **lacks norms** and is removed from social control. In addition, individuals shed their identity and **act as a group**. This absolves individuals of any guilt for the actions of the group. Nonetheless, a crowd seldom does anything beyond what individuals would do; and its violence is directed against a definite target. In addition to crowds, collective behavior is found in **rumors, fashions, fads** and **crazes**, in **publics** and **public opinion**.

Theorists have offered a variety of explanations for collective behavior. **LeBon** speculated that in crowds, individuals forgot their **rational faculties** and acted like savages who were suggestible and easily led by the example of others. Herbert **Blumer** states that **contagion** in a crowd results from a reflex chain reaction (contagion theory). Others maintain that collective behavior brings out into the open feelings already present in the individual members of the crowd (**convergence** theory); or that collective behavior is governed by norms that emerge spontaneously to fit the situation (**emergent norm** theory). The contagion and convergence theories assume that the crowd acts as one; the emergent norm theory recognizes the possibility of a variety of opinions, but dissenters remain silent, giving the illusion that the crowd acts as one.

A. FILL IN THE BLANKS:

1. Collective behavior takes place without _____ direction from the _____ _____ of society.
2. Additional characteristics of collective behavior are: it is: _____, _____, _____, and
_____.
3. Collective behavior is prevalent during times of _____
_____ _____.
4. A crowd is a _____ collection of people who respond to the same _____.
5. Crowds may be _____, _____, _____,
and _____.

6. In a crowd, people develop a_____ _____, shed their_____, and create new_____of acceptable behavior.

7. Although a crowd acts as a group, absolving individuals of any_____, the crowd will not go beyond what any individual would_____and its violence is directed against a definite _____.

8. Additional forms of collective behavior include,_____, _____, _____, _____, and_____opinion.

9. That people act like savages in crowds, imitating others, and being easily led was the opinion of_____.

10. A modern version of the contagion theory is offered by _____ _____.

11. The three most accepted theories of collective behavior are: _____, _____, and _____ _____.

B. CHAPTER OVERVIEW

Another form of collective behavior is to be found in **publics**. A public is a scattered collection of people who share a **common interest** or a concern about an issue, or who are affected by a common occurrence. Whereas **emotion** is the bond that holds a **crowd** together, **intellect** holds a public together. A public is dispersed, and only a few members of a public are able to communicate. Publics are **temporary**, and their composition changes quickly. They are **unstructured**, united by the **mass media**, and more characteristic of complex societies than of simple ones.

Publics give rise to **public opinion**. Public opinion is a generic term that refers to the **attitude** or judgment of a **large number of people** on a **specific issue**. It is the dominant opinion, or the position taken by a large public, on a particular issue. Again, public opinion has **special meaning** in a **complex society** with mass tendencies. In traditional societies, conflicting issues seldom arise, and since such societies tend to be nondemocratic, leaders are less concerned with the opinions of the people. The strongest influence on public opinion is exerted by the mass media.

Public opinion is sometimes **manipulated** by certain groups in society. One way of manipulating public opinion is through **propaganda** that is a deliberate attempt to persuade an individual to accept a particular belief, or to make a certain choice, uncritically.

Propaganda gives a **one-sided interpretation** to an issue, or shows only the good side of it, thus distorting the information available to the public. **Censorship**, on the other hand, deletes all or parts of the information available to the public. Many institutions use censorship--the government and the military, families, even business concerns and the mass media.

B. FILL IN THE BLANKS:

1. A public is a scattered_____of people who_____a common interest or are _____by a common event.
2. The element holding a public together is_____.
3. Publics are _____, _____, and their_____changes rapidly.
4. Publics are more characteristic of _____than of_____societies.
5. Publics give rise to_____ _____.
6. The dominant opinion of a large public is_____ _____.
7. Public opinion is less important in_____societies because_____issues seldom arise.
8. Certain groups in society manipulate public opinion through_____and_____.
9. Propaganda gives a _____interpretation to an issue.
10. Censorship _____information altogether.

C. CHAPTER OVERVIEW

Social movements consist of **collective behavior** that has as its goal the **alteration** of some aspect of the **social system**. During periods of rapid social change, people look for a **systematic** way of **interpreting** emerging perspectives. At such times, they are **receptive to ideologies**, that are systems of beliefs (doctrines) providing a basis for collective action. Ideologies **explain** why things are as they are; they **reinforce** the feelings of believers; and **direct** believers to action that will result in social change. Unfortunately, ideologies sometimes **distort** facts, and make their followers "true believers" blindly loyal to them.

Social movements are relatively **long lived**. They involve a significant number of people who share the underlying ideology. They are directed at a specific goal. And if they are successful, they are

institutionalized, i. e. they become permanent fixtures in the society.

Conditions that promote the **rise** of social movements include: **rapid social change**; feelings of **alienation** or normlessness on the part of individuals resulting from the unresponsiveness of the existing social structures; **relative deprivation**, that is, a desire on the part of some groups for the advantages enjoyed by other groups; **rising expectations**, or the fact that, having achieved some benefits, further aspirations are being blocked by existing social structures; and **downward mobility**, or loss of former status and wealth.

The two social movements that have had the most influence on societies have been the **revolutionary** and the **reform** movements. Reform movements attempt to alter some aspect of the social structure without overturning the entire structure. Often they seek to correct parts of a system that has strayed from its original pur-pose. Revolutionary movements attempt to supplant an entire social system with a new one. In a **nationalistic** revolutionary movement, a predominantly foreign government is overthrown and replaced with a native one. n a **class** revolutionary movement, one ruling class is substituted for another. **Change-resistant** movements reflect the belief that change occurs too rapidly. These movements want to protect the status quo from reform movements.

C. FILL IN THE BLANKS:

1. Social movements are _____of collective behavior with the goal of_____some aspect of the social system.
2. In times of rapid social change, people are receptive to

_____.

3. Systems of beliefs, or doctrines, are called _____.
4. The functions of ideologies include _____,_____
___, and _____toward action.
5. Social movements that are successful be-
come_____.
6. The characteristics of social movements include: they are
_____, they involve _____ _____, and they are
_____at a specific goal.
7. Among the conditions that promote the rise of social movements are: rapid_____ _____, feelings of_____, relative _____and rising_____.

8. The two social movements that have had the most influence on societies in recent times have been: the_____and the_____.

9. Revolutionary movements may be_____or _____movements.

10. The movement that tries to protect the status quo from change perceived as too rapid is_____.

TERMS TO REMEMBER

alienation: A feeling of powerlessness and insecurity, of not belonging in society, producing boredom and meaninglessness. Alienation provides a fertile ground for social movements and is characteristic of people in mass society.

censorship: A method of control used to limit the information available to the public.

change-resistant movement: A social movement reflecting the discontent of people who believe that change is occurring too rapidly and want to stop it.

class revolutionary movement: A revolutionary social movement in which one ruling class is replaced with another in the same society.

collective behavior: Type of behavior that tends to occur in crowds, mobs, fashions, fads, crazes, rumors, panics, and also in publics, public opinion, and social movements. It is characteristic of a collectivity of people who are responding to a common stimulus under conditions that are usually temporary, unstable, unstructured, and unpredictable so that existing norms do not apply.

nationalistic revolutionary movement: A revolutionary social movement in which a predominantly foreign government is over-thrown and replaced with a native one.

propaganda: A deliberate attempt to persuade people to uncritically accept a particular belief or to make a certain choice.

public and public opinion: Persons in society who are geographically dispersed but who share a common interest, express that interest, and know that others are aware of their interest. The totality of opinions, attitudes, and judgments expressed by publics.

HOW MUCH DO YOU RECALL? TEST YOUR KNOWLEDGE

MULTIPLE CHOICE QUESTIONS:

1. Collective behavior is often precipitated by:
    a. anomaly
    b. rapid social change
    c. deviant behavior
    c. fear of the future

2. Which is **not** a theory of collective behavior?
    a. Contagion
    b. Alienation
    c. Convergent
    d. Emergent norm

3. Which is **not** a characteristic of crowd behavior?
    a. Individuals maintain their identity
    b. Development of a common mood
    c. Behavior according to previously established norms
    d. Temporary

4. Which is false of communication?
    a. It is fundamental to culture building
    b. Communication on a large scale hinders change.
    c. It was greatly broadened by the inventions of writing and the printing press
    d. Direct communication resulted in a dramatic change in the structure of society

5. A scattered collection of people who share a common interest or a concern about an issue is a(n):
    a. group
    b. crowd
    c. public
    d. audience

6. Attempts to persuade the individual to accept a particular belief, or to make a specific choice, uncritically, include:
   a. public relations and advertising
   b. sales, sales promotion, and political campaigns
   c. propaganda
   d. all of the above

7. Which is **not** a form of collective behavior?
   a. Fashions
   b. Rumors
   c. Dining out with a friend
   d. Panic

8. The convergence theory:
   a. is the most accepted by social scientists
   b. maintains that people "catch" a certain behavior by being near others
   c. holds that being in a collectivity brings out into the open feelings already present in the individual
   d. is more logical than the contagion theory

9. Contagion theories:
   a. describe some kinds of crowd behavior, but not others
   b. assume that a collective situation brings together similar people
   c. state that new rules arise in collective situations
   d. assume that collective behavior is rational

10. A temporary collection of people gathered in the same place at the same time becomes a crowd when they:
    a. interact on a face-to-face basis
    b. respond to a common stimulus
    c. are personally acquainted with each other
    d. have the same thing in mind as to how to behave

11. Crowds may engage in unpredictable behavior because:
    a. they are temporary
    b. individuals can remain anonymous
    c. individuals are unpredictable
    d. they are temporary **AND** individuals are anonymous,

12. Publics and public opinion:
    a. are more characteristic of complex societies than of simple ones
    b. are more frequent in totalitarian societies than in democratic ones
    c. express the values of leaders of society
    d. have special meanings in traditional societies where conflicting issues are common

13. Censorship:
    a. is the same as propaganda
    b. gives a one-sided interpretation of an issue
    c. deletes all or parts of information
    d. is the opposite of propaganda

14. Which is **NOT** an element of a social movement?
    a. It has a specific perspective and ideology
    b. It involves no orientation toward action
    c. It has a strong sense of idealism and solidarity
    d. It involves a significant number of people

15. Collective behavior is:
    a. rather unstructured
    b. well planned
    c. based on regular norms
    d. individual behavior multiplied

16. Collective behavior:
    a. completely lacks structure
    b. has some connection with social factors
    c. is always disorganized
    d. none of the above

17. Social scientists are interested in collective behavior because it is:
    a. so predictable
    b. not tied to social factors
    c. often the basis of important social change
    d. reflective of purely animal behavior

18. The crowd at a religious revival meeting is:
   a. casual
   b. acting
   c. expressive
   d. disorganized

19. Violent crowd behavior:
   a. has no limits in its antisocial nature
   b. always goes against the wishes of individual members
   c. is generally random
   d. is usually temporary

20. Many listeners to a 1938 science-fiction radio program believed that Martians were really invading the Earth. They fled into the streets in panic. We would call their behavior
   a. fashion
   b. rational-legal behavior
   c. fantasy
   d. none of the above
   e. all of the above

CHAPTER 11

Ideologies and Their Consequences

In this chapter, you will learn

1. that the underpinnings of social movements consist of ideologies;
2. that political ideologies direct economic behavior as well;
3. the differences between autocratic and democratic ideologies;
4. about the dominant totalitarian ideology of the right and the social movements it spawned;
5. about the dominant totalitarian ideology of the left and the social movements that followed;
6. the precepts of the democratic ideology;
7. about such sub-ideologies of democracy as capitalism and democratic socialism.

TOPICAL OUTLINE

I. THE ROLE OF IDEOLOGY IN SOCIAL MOVEMENTS
    A. Characteristics
    B. Political Ideology
II. AUTOCRATIC IDEOLOGIES
    A. Authoritarianism and Totalitarianism
        1. Totalitarianism of the Right: Fascism and Nazism
            a. Elements of Fascism
        2. Totalitarianism of the Left: Communism
            a. The Marxist Foundation
            b. Historical Prediction Through the Method of the Dialectic
            c. Communism and the former USSR
            d. Communism in Disarray
            e. The Eastern Bloc
            f. China
III. DEMOCRACY
    A. Democratic Capitalism
    B. Socialism
        1. Democratic Socialism

A. CHAPTER OVERVIEW

Much of our **social world** is based on **ideas, concepts, and symbols** that explain and justify the way things are, as well as the way things ought to be. When such ideas are systematic, rational, intelligible, and organized into a logical pattern of thought, they are said to be **ideologies**. More completely, an ideology is a **value or belief system** that is **accepted as fact** or truth by some group. It consists of **sets of attitudes** toward the institutions and processes of society and provides the believer with a **picture of the world** as it is and as it should be, thus making a complex world easily understandable.

Our lives are guided by a number of ideologies. However, political and economic ideologies have special functions, characteristics, and consequences. They tend to **arise** during periods of **crisis** and among those to whom the dominant world view has become unacceptable. Some are very **comprehensive** (totalitarian), others are **partial**. They are **abstract**, being a model derived from one person's perception of reality. They are **reductionist**, in that they reduce what is complex into an understandable form. And they are **meaningless outside** of **social movements**.

The **functions** of ideologies include: making the governors acceptable to the governed (**lending government** a **justification** without which it could not function); providing a **cognitive structure**, a system through which the world is perceived, understood, and interpreted, thus helping people avoid insecurity and strain; **guiding specific behaviors** and attitudes of individuals and groups; and serving as a **vital force** in life, offering a sense of mission and purpose, and a commitment to action.

Political ideology refers to concepts dealing with questions as to **who** will be the rulers, **how** they will be selected, and by **what** principles they will govern. It is meant to **persuade** and **counter** opposing views, and to affect some major value. It has a **program** for the retention, reform, or abolition of social institutions. It partially rationalizes group interest. It is **normative, ethical, and moral** in tone and content. And it is a part of a broader belief system whose properties it shares.

Ideologies are **not monolithic**, but contain differences within them; people are **socialized** into the **dominant** political ideology of their society, and tend to act accordingly; and most people hold **conflicting** ideologies at the same time.

A. FILL IN THE BLANKS:

1. Ideologies are _____ of ideas that are _____ , _____ , and _____.

2. Ideologies consist of _____ ___ _____ toward societal institutions and processes.

3. Ideologies provide the believer with a _____ of the world as it is and as it _____ _____.

148

4. Political and economic ideologies tend to arise during_____ of _____and among those to whom the _____ideology has become_____.

5. Ideologies are also described as being _____or partial, _____, and_____.

6. The functions of ideologies include: lending_____, providing a cognitive_____, offering a sense of _____ ___ _____to life.

7. The most important concept in political ideology deals with the questions of:_____, how will the governors be_____and by what_____they will govern.

8. Political ideology is meant to _____and counter_____views.

9. Political ideology offers a program for either_____, _____, or_____some major institution.

10. There are differences within ideologies; thus they are not_____. In addition, people tend to act according to the ideology into which they were_____. Finally, most people hold_____ideologies simultaneously.

B. CHAPTER OVERVIEW

Autocracy is an ideology based on the belief that **government** should be **in the hands of one individual or group** who has **supreme power** over the people of a society. Through history, autocracy has had many forms; but in modern times, traditional autocracy has been replaced by ideologies of the right and of the left that we call **totalitarian**. These ideologies are based on modern technology and mass legitimation. They came into existence when what were thought to be short-lived dictatorships became permanent regimes. Some **common features** of totalitarian regimes include: the official ideology expresses a **revolt** against present society, and **idealistic hopes** for a future, more perfect society and the ideology is **totalist**: it attempts to reform the total individual and prescribes a life-style with implications in all spheres of life. Totalitarian regimes maintain a **single** party functioning as the organization through which the ideology is kept alive; the head of the party is a **leader (dictator)** or an **oligarchy** (small elite) who interprets the ideology to the masses. The state has a **secret police**, controls the **mass media,** controls all **arms**, and centrally plans and controls the **economy**.

Fascism and Nazism are two totalitarian ideologies of the **right**. Fascism came to power in Italy in 1922, and Nazism emerged in Germany a decade later. Most of the differences between the two ideologies are due to the different **personalities** of the two leaders, Benito Mussolini in Italy and Adolf Hitler in Germany.

The principal elements of the fascist outlook include: a **distrust** of **reason**, the **denial** of basic **human equality**, a code of behavior based on **violence** and distortion of truth,

149

government by the **elite**, totalitarianism, racism, imperialism, and opposition to international law and order. Fascist principles of organization and control are applied to the economy of fascist regimes. The economy is divided into state-controlled associations of capital and labor, and the ultimate mediator is the one-party state. The most virulent forms of fascism were eliminated with the defeat of the Axis powers in World War II. However, fascistic tendencies can be observed in a number of nations today.

Communism is a totalitarian ideology of the **left**. It is based on very old ideals of egalitarianism, but its modern expression is to be found in the conditions following the Industrial Revolution. The principal author of communist ideology was Karl Marx who speculated that people's conditions and beliefs were determined by **economic relationships**; that in fact all relationships in life rested on an economic base. In addition, change was constant in societies, and it proceeded through a number of struggles. In societies that were at the capitalist stage of economic development, the struggle was between the **bourgeoisie** (owners of the means of production) and the **proletariat** (industrial workers). Marx tried to predict historical outcomes through a tool of analysis called the **dialectic**, a method of questions and answers in which a position is stated, criticized until the opposite position is taken, and finally a middle position between the two opposites is attained. But Marx was **wrong** in predicting the **demise of capitalism** and the victory of the proletariat. In spite of this, today almost half of the world lives under regimes that consider themselves Marxist. Among the most powerful of these are the U.S.S.R. and the People's Republic of China. The economies of these nations are centrally and rigidly planned, and the intent remains to abolish private property and nationalize the means of production. While these nations have been much less successful in producing consumer goods, they have attained an important status on the world stage, although neither has achieved that **ultimate goal**--a **classless** society.

B. FILL IN THE BLANKS:

1. Autocracy is an ideology based on the belief that government should be in the hands of _____.

2. In modern times, traditional autocracies have been replaced by regimes of the_____and the _____that are called _____.

3. Some of the common features of totalitarian regimes include_____against present society, hope for a_____society, prescription for a lifestyle in_____of life.

4. Totalitarian regimes maintain a_____party through which the ideology is _____ _____; the leader or oligarchy _____the ideology to the masses.

5. The two totalitarian ideologies of the right are_____, which originated in_____in 19__; and_____, which arose in_____a decade later.

6. The principal elements of fascist ideology include: a_____
of reason, a denial of _____ _____, and behavior based on a code
of_____.

7. In a fascist regime, the economy is divided into state-controlled associations
of_____and_____; the ultimate mediator is the_____.

C. CHAPTER OVERVIEW

Democracy, the ideology diametrically opposed to autocracy, is an **ideology, a philosophy, a theory, and a political system**. Among the **assumptions** and principles of democracy are: that the **individual** is **valuable** in addition to being free, rational, moral, equal, and in possession of certain rights. Another **central element** of democratic philosophy is the principle that the only **legitimate basis for rule is peoples' consent** to be ruled. Thus, the state is merely a trustee of the people and has no authority or purpose except as assigned by the people.

Capitalism is considered a **subideology**, or a blend of political and economic ideas that are mutually reinforcing. Classical capitalism is **based** on the ideas of Adam Smith who, in **The Wealth of Nations** (1776), maintained a belief in the private ownership of property, in the existence of a profit motive, in the dynamics of a free market; and in the importance of competition. The private ownership of property is beneficial, according to Smith, first, because the power it creates is better in the hands of many individuals rather than concentrated in the state, and second, because the economic growth of the society is attained more easily if each individual uses personal incentive to get ahead. Smith also believed that the free market system worked smoothly, as if an "invisible hand" were directing it.

Classical capitalism has undergone many transformations, and today's economies are usually called **mixed economies** in which the government interferes, competition has been diluted by the existence of private or state monopolies, and in which the **profit motive,** though still dominant, also can lead to bankruptcies and failures. In order to work perfectly, capitalism must exist in an environment of perfect equality of opportunity. But for a variety of reasons such equality of opportunity is difficult to attain; so nations with capitalistic mixed economies have adopted **welfare systems** to help those who are victimized by the system. But such systems are seldom completely successful.

Although socialism refers to an economic concept, **democratic socialism** is an ideology that rests on both economic and political assumptions. Its most fundamental assumption is that participation in political decision making should be extended to economic decision making. Thus, voters should be able to control their economic future as they do their political future. In all other respects, democratic socialism accepts and supports the democratic ideology, both in theory and in practice. Democratic **socialism** assumes that the **state** and its government are the **necessary instruments** through which people can achieve and maintain their objectives, some of which are: holding most **property in the name of the people**, especially all major **industries, utilities, and transportation**; limiting the accumulation of private property; and **regulating the economy**.

The key difference between democratic **capitalism** and democratic **socialism** is the way **property is held** in a society. Democratic socialists argue that by ensuring everyone of economic security, they are making liberty possible for everyone. Democratic capitalists argue that only when property is held privately are people free to compete for rewards. Socialism attempts to bring together the best elements of Western civilization. The dilemma it faces is how to avoid the growth of the power of the state at the expense of individual freedom.

C. FILL IN THE BLANKS:

1. Some of the assumptions of democracy include: the_____ of the individual, and that individuals are_____, _____, _____and in possession of specific_____.
2. A central element of the democratic philosophy is the principle that the only legitimate basis for rule is_____ _____to be ruled.
3. The state is merely a_____of the people and has no authority except as_____by the people.
4. Capitalism is a_____, a blend of_____ and _____ and_____ideas.
5. Classical capitalism is based on the ideas of_____who wrote _____ _____ __ _____in_____.
6. The principles of classical capitalism include: the ownership of_____, the _____motive, a_____market, and _____.
7. Today's economies are called_____because they include government_____, a diluted form of_____, and a profit motive that can lead to_____.
8. To work perfectly, capitalism should exist in an environment of _____ _____.
9. The most fundamental assumption of democratic socialism is that_____decision making should be extended to_____decision making.
10. Socialism assumes that the instrument through which people attain their goals is the_____and its_____.
11. The key difference between democratic capitalism and democratic socialism is the way_____is held.

TERMS TO REMEMBER

authoritarianism: type of autocracy (see below) in which power is held by an absolute monarch, dictator, or small elite. Power is limited to the political sphere.

autocracy: An ideology directly opposed to democracy, in which government rests in the hands of one individual or group who holds supreme power over the people.

communism: A political and economic ideology whose ultimate goal is total government control of the economy and total income redistribution, leading to the creation of a classless society.

democracy: An ideology, philosophy, theory, and political system assuming the basic value of the individual, as well his or her rationality, morality, equality, and possession of specific rights.

democratic capitalism: A blend of political and economic ideology whose tenets include the private ownership of property, the profit motive, a free market economy, and competition. The function of government in this system is to ensure that the economic game is played fairly.

democratic socialism: A blend of political and economic ideology whose chief assumption is that participation in political decision making should be extended to economic decision making. The function of the government in this system is to control and guide the economy for the benefit of the voters who elected it.

fascism: A totalitarian ideology of the right that became prominent in various nations beginning in Italy under Benito Mussolini.

ideology: A system of ideas, values, beliefs, and attitudes that a society or groups within a society share and accept as true.

nazism: The German version of fascism that flourished under the leadership of Adolf Hitler.

totalitarianism: A type of autocracy of the left or of the right, characterized by a totalist ideology, a single party, a government-controlled secret police, and a monopoly by the ruling elite over mass communications, weapons, and the economy.

HOW MUCH DO YOU RECALL? TEST YOUR KNOWLEDGE

MULTIPLE CHOICE QUESTIONS:

1. A system of ideas, values, beliefs, and attitudes shared by members of a society and accepted as true by them is a(n):
   a. doctrine
   b. religion
   c. philosophy
   d. ideology

2. One of the basic assumptions of the ideology of democracy is:
   a. the importance of the collectivity
   b. the value of the individual
   c. equality of results
   d. the pursuit of happiness

3. Autocracy may be defined as:
   a. the ideology most directly opposed to democracy
   b. the ideology that holds that government should be in the hands of the people
   c. a corollary of democracy
   d. a precursor of democracy

4. Totalitarian regimes:
   a. are the equivalent of the autocracies of the past
   b. can exist within democracies
   c. are kinds of autocracies based on modern technology and mass legitimation
   d. are short-lived dictatorships

5. The goal of communism was:
   a. to prohibit any evidence of capitalist market activity
   b. to reverse the class system of societies
   c. private ownership of the means of production
   d. total income redistribution and ultimately a classless society

6. In most societies, ownership of property takes one of three forms:
   a. restricted, guarded, and private
   b. esthetic, visible, tangible
   c. communal, private, public
   d. ambiguous, hermetic, contraceptive

7. What does one call property owned by the state in the name of the people?
   a. public
   b. private
   c. common-law
   d. communal

8. The "invisible hand" refers to:
   a. a feature of Adam Smith's *The Wealth of Nations*
   b. the belief in God exhibited by the Puritans
   c. the fact that prayer results in help
   d. a belief in ghosts prevalent in the early Middle Ages

9. Laissez-faire:
   a. has nothing to do with economic theory
   b. is the rallying cry of the Gay Liberation Movement
   c. was Karl Marx's exhortation to the workers of the world
   d. is the French word Adam Smith used to mean that government should keep its hands off the economy

10. The private ownership of property was deemed beneficial to the society because it:
    a. diffused power
    b. used the incentive motive
    c. was the American way
    d. only a and b

11. The fundamental assumption of democratic socialism is that:
    a. participation in political decision making should be extended to religious leaders
    b. the Socialist party must be in command of the economy
    c. participation in political decision making should be extended to economic decision making
    d. it is not necessary for everyone in a society to work

12. Which is **not** a characteristic of the fascist ideology?
    a. Distrust of reason
    b. Concern with basic equality of humankind
    c. Code of behavior based on violence
    d. Government by elite

13. The "dialectic" is a tool of analysis associated with the work of:
   a. Karl Marx
   b. Adam Smith
   c. Benito Mussolini
   d. Adolf Hitler

14. In its most dogmatic aspect, the communist ideology focused on the following goals:
   a. abolition of all private property
   b. class warfare
   c. the dictatorship of the proletariat
   d. all of the above
   e. none of the above

15. Karl Marx predicted that the revolution would occur in:
   a. the United States
   b. Russia
   c. Germany
   d. Great Britain

16. One mistake Marx made was that he underestimated the workers':
   a. ignorance
   b. nationalism
   c. poverty
   d. laziness

17. Political ideology deals with:
   a. matters of ruler selection and principles of rule
   b. parties
   c. economics
   d. none of the above

18. MacIver believed that the main function of political ideology (myth complex) was:
   a. making people feel free
   b. secure the will of the people
   c. give legitimate authority to the government in power
   d. fool the people some of the time

CHAPTER 12

GOVERNMENT: THE INSTITUTION AND THEORIES

In this chapter, you will learn

1.   what are pivotal institutions;
2.   the reason for the establishment of the institution of govern ment;
3.   the purpose and functions of government;
4.   the importance of legitimacy and authority in the exercise of political power, as well as the types of authority;
5.   the differences between the state and government;
6.   the definition of a nation state.

TOPICAL OUTLINE

I. INSTITUTIONS
II. THE PIVOTAL INSTITUTION OF GOVERNMENT
    A. Purpose of Government
    B. Functions of Government
III. POLITICAL POWER: LEGITIMACY AND AUTHORITY
    A. Legitimacy
    B. Authority
        1. Types of Legitimate Authority
            a. Traditional Authority
            b. Legal-Rational Authority
            c. Charismatic Authority
IV. THE STATE
    A. The Relationship of State and Its Government
    B. Theoretical views of the State
V. THE NATION-STATE
        1. Nationalism

A. CHAPTER OVERVIEW

Government is an **institution** that arises out of the need for **social order**. In turn, social order is a by-product of group life and is implemented through various means of **social control**. Social control is **the process** by which the **group**, whether it be society or smaller groups within it, **induces or forces** the **individual** to

157

behave in a designated way. To exert social control, it is necessary to possess **power**. Social control that is **institutionalized**, that is, that is sufficiently surrounded with customs and traditions to set a pattern, is called **government**. Government **includes** a system of **values, norms, laws** and general **patterns of behavior** that **legitimize** the acquisition and exercise of power.

In **simple societies**, social order may be maintained through **moral control** that is internalized cultural learning acquired through socialization. In a **complex society**, social order can be maintained only if moral control is supplemented by **political control** exerted by forces outside the individual. People invest a person or entity with the authority to exercise political control. When and how such political control is to be exercised, as well as by whom, is determined by the various processes of government.

Thus, the **most important function of government** is to **implement social control**. Government also **protects** its citizens from external threats; **plans** and maintains facilities and activities involving large portions of the population; **regulates** the economy; builds highways, funds schools, maintains national parks, and so on. Among the effects of government that were neither intended nor foreseen were party machines that were common in the past.

A. FILL IN THE BLANKS:

1. Government is an institution that arises out of the need for_____ _____.

2. Social order is a result of _____ life and is implemented by _____ _____.

3. To exert social control, one needs to have_____.

4. The process by which a group induces an individual to behave in a certain way is called_____ _____.

5. Government may be defined as social control that is_____.

6. Government legitimizes the acquisition and exercise of_____.

7. In simple societies, social order may be maintained through_____ alone.

8. In complex societies, social order must be supplemented by_____ _____.

9. Various processes of government determine _____, and by _____ political control is to be exercised.

10. In addition to implementing social control, government also_____citizens from external threats, _____ facilities,_____the economy, etc.

B. CHAPTER OVERVIEW

Power is **central** to the political process because in order to exert social control, it is necessary to have the power to do so. One **definition** of power is that one party in a social relationship will **carry out his/her own** will **despite resistance**. Power is important in a variety of social interactions, and it can be asserted in a number of ways--through **rewards, coercion, or influence**.

Political power is power exercised by the **state** through its government. The **state** is the **abstract** representation of the political system of a society. The state has the **authority** to employ **force** to **implement social control**, and its authority is legitimate. That is, when the members of a society accept the use of power on the part of an individual or entity as right and proper, that power is considered **legitimate**. When power is used illegally and **illegitimately**, it is termed **coercion**. When it is used legally and legitimately, it is called authority.

Authority, then, refers to power over, or **control of**, individuals that is socially accepted as **right and proper**. Authority derives from a number of sources summarized by the social thinker Max Weber as: **traditional**, in which legitimization derives from the past and authority is accepted because it has always been so; **legal/rational**, in which authority is established on rules arrived at in a rational manner and is based on the rule of law; and **charismatic**, or embodied in the person of an exceptional leader.

B. FILL IN THE BLANKS:

1. An element central to the political process is_____.
2. One definition of power is the ability of one party in a relation-ship to carry out his/her will_____.
3. Power can be asserted through_____, _____, and_____, and is and can be recognized in a variety of _____.
4. Political power is exercised by the_____through its_____.

159

5. The state has the_____to implement social control because it has a monopoly on force.
6. The state's authority is_____.
7. Legitimate power is power that members of a society accept as being_____and_____.
8. Legitimate power is called_____.
9. Illegitimate and illegal power is called_____.
10. The sources of authority may be summarized as being _____, and_____.

C. CHAPTER OVERVIEW

Government is the institution that develops because of the need to maintain social order in a society. Government is a process that **includes the group of people who exercise political power**. The state, on the other hand, is the abstract embodiment, the symbol, of the institution. The **state is permanent**; **government**, as the operational arm of the state, is **temporary**. The state is a political unit; and its government consists of individuals who are organized to exercise structured political control within the society. Membership in the state is compulsory for those who live within its territorial limits; and its political control is complete. The basic **components** of the state are **territory**, **population**, **government**, and **sovereignty**.

The interpretation of the relationship between government and the governed, and the concept of legitimacy in political affairs depend on two opposing points of view. Thomas Hobbes, in *The Leviathan* (1651), speculated that people accepted the authority of government by forming a **social contract** in which they relinquished a measure of individual liberty in return for protection and social order because it was difficult living in the **state of nature** in which every person fought against every other person. John Locke, in *Two Treatises of Government* (1690), disagreed with Hobbes that life in the state of nature was violent. Rather, life was guided by reason and people entered into a social contract because it was the **reasonable** thing to do: law and order would be administered by impartial institutions, and government would consist of known laws. Locke also thought that government should be **limited**, should rest on the **consent** of the governed, and its **purpose** should be to protect the property and rights of individuals.

Contemporary views on the state include **functionalism** and the **conflict** theory. Functionalists are the theoretical descendants of Hobbes who **perceive** the **state** as a functional institution **necessary for maintaining law and order**, providing the ultimate source of arbitration, an orderly allocation of resources, economic coordination, and acting as a vehicle for interaction with other states. Conflict theorists look to the French philosopher Jean-Jacques Rousseau, who also disagreed with Hobbes, in their belief that before the emergence of the state--that occurred to protect the position of the privileged--people lived as **"noble savages"** who only began to fight when the notion of private property developed. Karl Marx agreed with Rousseau, believing that all but the most primitive societies consisted of at least two classes of which one dominated and exploited the other through social institutions. The **state**, in **Marx's view**, was an instrument in the **service of the ruling class.**

C. FILL IN THE BLANKS:

1. Government is the _____that includes the _____who exercise political power.

2. The state is the_____embodiment, the_____ _____, of the institution of government.

3. The state is_____, the government_____.

4. The basic components of the state are_____, _____, and_____ _____.

5. Two opposing views on the relationship of government to the governed are presented by _____and_____.

6. The author of *The Leviathan* speculated that people accepted _____ _____because life in the_____ ___ ___ was "nasty, brutish, solitary, and short."

7. In the contract, people relinquished some liberty in exchange for _____and_____ _____.

8. The author of *Two Treatises of Government* maintained that life in the state of nature was guided by_____and people entered into the_____contract because it was the_____ thing to do.

9. Some of the ideas of the above author reflected in the American Constitution are:_____government, government resting on the_____of the governed, and offering _____of property.

10. Contemporary views of the origin of the state include _____and_____theory.

161

D. CHAPTER OVERVIEW

The growth in size and complexity of societies led people to seek political organization first in **kinship clans**, then in **tribes**, later in **city-states**, and finally in **nation-states**. The **nation** is an abstract concept symbolizing a **culture group** residing within the territory of the political state. It is the spirit of nationhood that makes a group of people a nation. The factors that help unify a people into a nation are: **geographic boundaries, commercial ties, a common language, loyalty to a common political entity** as well as a **common history, literature, and a sense of a common future**.

Sovereignty is the recognition that the government of a particular country has supreme authority over its own subjects and that the country is **impermeable and impenetrable** by other nation states. Sovereignty refers to the status of nation-states in the **international** arena, and foreign policy is waged by each nation-state to maintain its sovereignty. Some commentators maintain that the concept is becoming obsolete because the nation-state is giving way to a new form of political organization; others say that claims to sovereignty have little meaning in an atomic age. But while sovereignty may have lost some relevance in Western Europe, it has **grown** in importance in nations of Asia, the Middle East, and Africa.

Nationalism is the **ideology** behind the nation state and has been essential in creating modern societies. Nationalism is a set of beliefs about the **superiority and uniqueness** of one's own nation and a defense of its interest above all others. It is **ethnocentrism** that cuts across all other loyalties to stress **loyalty to the national group**. The ultimate goal of the social, political, and economic efforts of the people are directed at the survival of the nation. Historically, nationalism is a movement dating to the second half of the 18th century and particularly following World War I, when a number of totalitarian regimes emerged. **Governments use nationalism** to insure internal allegiance, and since nationalistic aims are reached through **military power**, nationalism is a contributing factor in the arms race.

162

D. FILL IN THE BLANKS:

1. People sought political organization in:_____,
_____,_____and_____.
2. A nation is an_____concept symbolizing a
_____residing within the territory of _____.
3. A group of people become a nation when they can feel the spirit
of_____.
4. The factors making up that spirit include:_____,
_____, a common_____ and_____
and a sense of a common_____.
5. Sovereignty is the recognition that the government of a particular country has _____ _____over its own
subjects and is_____ and_____ by other
nations.
6. Foreign policy is waged by each nation-states to maintain
its_____.
7. The concept of sovereignty has grown in importance in the
nations of_____, the_____,
and_____.
8. Nationalism is the_____behind the nation-state
which has been essential in creating _____ _____.
9. Nationalism is a set of_____about the
_____ and_____of one's own nation, and a
defense of its_____above all others.
10. Historically, nationalism dates to the_____ _____of
the_____century and especially following_____ ___.

TERMS TO REMEMBER

charismatic authority: According to Max Weber, a type of
authority based on the leadership of a person with charisma. A
charismatic leader is thought to possess special gifts of a
magnetic, fascinating, and extraordinary nature.

legal-rational authority: According to Weber, a type of authority
accepted by members of society because it is based on rational
methods and laws, and is exerted for their benefit.

nation: A culture group residing within the territory of a political
state.

nationalism: The ideology behind the nation state. A set of beliefs about the superiority of one's own nation and a defense of its interest above all others.

politics: The forces that make up and direct the government of the state, its policies, and its actions.

power: The probability that one individual in a social relationship will carry out his own will despite resistance. The ability of one person or group to direct the behavior of another person or group in a desired direction, under the ultimate, though not always obvious, threat of force.

rule of law: A constitutional principle holding that those in public authority derive, maintain, and exercise their powers on the basis of specific laws, and not on the basis of their personal power.

state: The formal, abstract symbol of government.

traditional authority: According to Weber, authority that is based on reverence for tradition.

HOW MUCH DO YOU RECALL? TEST YOUR KNOWLEDGE

MULTIPLE CHOICE QUESTIONS

1.   "The probability that one actor within a social relationship will be in a position to carry out his own will despite resistance" is a definition of:
        a. the top echelons of management
        b. leadership abilities
        c. power
        d. stardom in the rock music industry

2.   Legal-rational authority is characteristic of:
        a. homogeneous societies
        b. traditional, agrarian societies
        c. urban industrial, developed societies
        d. totalitarian societies

3. The difference between government and state is that:
   a. government is a symbol and state is the process
   b. government is a process that includes the people who exercise political power
   c. the state is an abstract symbol of the political institution
   d. both b and c

4. The most important function of government is to:
   a. provide social welfare
   b. implement social control
   c. exercise total control
   d. regulate human life in society

5. The basic components of the state include all but which of the following?
   a. territory
   b. population
   c. armed services
   d. sovereignty

6. The functionalist school maintains that the state:
   a. protects the rights of the privileged
   b. is on the way out
   c. is an extension of the "state of nature"
   d. is a human invention necessary to maintain order

7. Pivotal institutions include:
   a. property, warfare, and the law
   b. the family, religion, and government
   c. faith, hope, and charity
   d. insane asylums, prisons, and public schools

8. Hitler led the German people by emotional speeches. He derived his authority from:
   a. God
   b. the law
   c. the Bible
   d. personal charisma

9. Functionalists approach the state as a tool to:
    a. maintain order
    b. protect the privileged few
    c. protect private property
    d. maintain the state of nature

10. Conflict theorists see the state's functions as:
    a. protecting the interest of the ruling elite only
    b. helping the poor and homeless
    c. bringing peace to its citizens
    d. directing the economy

11. Marx believed that the state would vanish when:
    a. the elite would work toward the good of the masses
    b. the lion would lie down with the lamb
    c. social classes ceased to exist
    d. all societies became capitalist

12. "My country, right or wrong" is an example of:
    a. nationalism
    b. legal-rational thinking
    c. an internationalist world view
    d. a reasoned approach to detente

13. A person affected by nationalism:
    a. identifies with a state's culture
    b. shares a state's interests and goals
    c. displays feelings of ethnocentrism
    d. all of the above
    e. none of the above

14. In order for power to be legitimate, a government must have:
    a. the ability to coerce agreement
    b. legitimate authority
    c. a charismatic leader
    d. a strong army

15. Legal-rational authority tends to be characteristic of:
    a. homogeneous, single-culture societies
    b. heterogeneous, multicultural societies
    c. simple agrarian societies
    d. Central American societies

16. In essence, people need government because:
    a. they live in groups and need a degree of order
    b. of their competitive nature
    c. they have not reached a sufficient amount of civilization to exist without it
    d. brute force is not sufficient to keep them in line

17. Political control:
    a. is internalized cultural learning
    b. is acquired through socialization
    c. is social control exerted by forces outside the individual
    d. takes the place of moral control in simple societies

18. Political power:
    a. appears only in capitalistic societies
    b. is power exercised by the state through its government
    c. characterizes all dictatorships
    d. belongs to a ruler in democratic regimes

19. The state has the following relationship to force:
    a. it shares it with the citizens
    b. it lacks it completely in a democracy
    c. it has a monopoly on it
    d. it gives it up to the people

CHAPTER 13

THE GOVERNMENT OF THE UNITED STATES OF AMERICA

In this chapter, you will learn

1. the historical sequence in the establishment of American political institutions, including the Constitutional Convention, the meaning of the Constitution, federalism, the principle of separation of powers, and checks and balances;
2. about the implications of the executive branch;
3. the weaknesses of the legislative branch;
4. the functions of the judicial branch;
5. the importance of limited government.

TOPICAL OUTLINE

I. AMERICAN POLITICAL INSTITUTIONS
    A. The Constitutional Convention
        1. Goals of the Constitutional Convention
        2. What Is A Constitution?
II. THE CONSTITUTION OF THE UNITED STATES
III. FEDERALISM
    A. How Federalism Has Worked
    B. Trend Toward Centralization
    C. Impact of Federal Government
IV. SEPARATION OF POWERS
    A. How Checks and Balances Work
    B. Criticism of the Separation of Powers
V. THE PRESIDENCY: THE EXECUTIVE BRANCH
    A. The Nature of the Presidency
        1. The Roles of the President
        2. The Presidency: The Person and the Office
VI. CONGRESS: THE LEGISLATIVE BRANCH
    A. The Issue of Representation
        1. Congressional Organization
        2. Congressional Committees
        3. Seniority Rule
        4. The Subordinate Role of Congress
VII. THE SUPREME COURT: THE JUDICIAL BRANCH
    A. The Court System
        1. Functions of the Judicial System
VIII. THE IMPORTANCE OF LIMITED GOVERNMENT

A. CHAPTER OVERVIEW

With the **exception** of political **parties**, all of the political institutions of the United States were **conceived** and delineated at the **Constitutional Convention of 1787**. It has been charged that the originators of the Constitution met to preserve the interests of their social class--propertied landowners--but the opinion now prevails that their chief **concern** was really to create a **government** that would **survive** and be **workable** and still serve the interests of all groups in society. **Constitutions** are instruments for establishing a framework for government. They **limit the power of the government** by stating the boundaries of its authority. They provide **specific procedures** for governmental **action**, and, by implication, **forbid** other action. Thus, the governed are guaranteed protection against possible arbitrary actions of the governors. The true ruler in such a framework is the law. This **"rule of law"** is an important principle of constitutionality. It holds that those in public authority **derive, maintain, and exercise** their powers on the basis of **laws** specifically drawn up. The four major constitutional principles of American government are: **federalism, separation of powers** and **checks and balances**; **judicial supremacy** and **limited government**.

Federalism may be defined as a **system** of distributing political power between a **central**, national government and the governments of the geographical regions into which the nation is divided. The allocation of power is outlined in the Constitution and may be altered only by a **constitutional amendment**. In theory, the federal system brings government closer to the people because state governments are not subordinate to the central government.

But federalism necessitates a vast **bureaucracy** in which various agencies quibble about authority and resources. There are also **inequities** in the way some state programs are administered, leading to the trend of letting the national government assume a larger share of responsibility. The principle of **separation of powers** is also prescribed by the Constitution. It provides for the **legislative, executive, and judicial** functions to be divided among three separate branches of government, one to **formulate and enact laws**, another to see that the laws are **carried out**, and a third to determine whether the laws are in **agreement** with the Constitution. Each branch is directly involved in the workings of the other two through the process of **checks and balances**. While the principle is criticized because the system is often cumbersome, unwieldy, and slow, the concern was for power to be shared and not allowing it to become concentrated in one branch.

A. FILL IN THE BLANKS:

1. Only_____ _____were not conceived and outlined at the _____ _____in 1787.

2. Constitutions are instruments for establishing a _____
for_____.
3. Constitutions_____the power of the government,
provide_____for government action, and they forbid other actions
by_____.
4. The most important principle of constitutionality is the_____ __ _____.
5. The four principles of the American Constitution are:

_____,_____ _____,_____ _____,
and_____ _____.
6. Federalism is a system of _____political power between
the_____government and the governments of the regions into which the
nation is divided.
7. The allocation of power is outlined in the_____and may be altered only
by_____amendment.
8. The disadvantages of federalism include a vast_____and the
_____with which state programs are administered.
9. The principle that the legislative, executive, and judicial functions of government be
separated is called_____ __ _____.
10. Each branch of government is directly involved in the working of the other two
through the process of_____ ____ _____.

B. CHAPTER OVERVIEW

There were no models for the Constitutional Convention to follow regarding an
executive branch or the office of the president. What finally emerged as the office of
the **chief executive** included these features: one chief executive; a four-year-term that
could be terminated only by death or impeachment; the electoral base to be
independent of Congress; and some constitutional powers independent of Congress,
the electors, the people, and the states. As for the **roles** of the chief executive, they
are: chief of state, chief legislator, chief administrator, chief diplomat or foreign policy
maker, party leader, and commander-in-chief of the armed forces.

The delegates also devised a system of government that included a **popular
representative assembly**, the House of Representatives. The House was to be the
forum for the people of the entire nation, while the **Senate** was to have the same
purpose for the states and minorities. The Constitution leaves the manner of election
of representatives up to the individual states. The state legislatures chose to divide the
states into **congressional districts** for election purposes. Districts must be reappor-
tioned every ten years after the census. Representation has not been perfect: studies
have shown that members of Congress do not necessarily represent the feelings of
most of their constituents, especially in the sphere of foreign relations and social
welfare. Congressional **organization**, with older members clinging to **tradition** and
demanding deference, and the powerful influence exerted by some committees, seems

to explain partially the ineffectiveness of Congress which is felt most acutely in the areas of foreign relations and military affairs. Most policy proposals tend to **originate in the executive branch** and from military and industrial pressure groups.

The **Supreme Court** was meant to represent a final bulwark against **majority tyranny** as well as a check on the representational aspect of Congress and the independent aspect of the presidency. **Judicial review** is the ability to judge the constitutionality of presidential and Congressional acts, as well as that of state legislation. Because of the federal type of government, the judicial system that has arisen in the United States is quite **complex**. It includes 50 sets of state judicial hierarchies, in addition to the federal judicial hierarchy. State courts, while not inferior to federal courts, have jurisdiction in cases arising out of state constitutions and state statutes, as well as out of the common law of each state. The judicial power to interpret and apply statutes to specific cases is, however, a lawmaking power itself. Judges possess a degree of choice that may be as great as that of other legislative bodies.

The principle of **limited government** is **basic to constitutionalism** because in the democratic tradition the purpose of a constitution is to limit the power of government. The very structure and processes of government express this principle. Further limitations on government are **embodied** in the **Bill of Rights** and particularly in the First Amendment.

B. FILL IN THE BLANKS:

1. The executive branch, as finally outlined by the Constitutional Convention, includes these features: one_____ _____, a _____-____ term, an_____electoral base, and some_____constitutional powers.
2. Among the roles of the president are: chief_____, chief_____, chief_____, chief_____, party_____, and _____ - __ _____of the armed forces.
3. The House of Representatives was intended to be a forum for the_____ _____.
4. According to the Constitution, representatives are elected in the manner chosen by the_____.
5. State legislatures divided states into_____ _____for elections.
6. Although constitutionally Congress had the potential for power, in reality its role has been_____to the executive branch.
7. Policy proposals that do not originate in the executive, do so from_____and_____ _____groups.
8. The Supreme Court was intended as a check on the_____ aspect of Congress and the_____aspect of the presidency.
9. Judicial review is the ability to judge the_____of presidential and Congressional_____as well as that of_____ _____.

10. The judicial system of the United States is very_____; state courts have jurisdiction in cases arising out of_____constitutions and statutes, as well as out of the_____ _____of their state.

11. The judicial power to interpret and apply statutes is a_____power in itself.

TERMS TO REMEMBER

checks and balances: The method resulting from the principle of separation of powers in which each branch of government is directly and indirectly involved in the workings of the other branches.

concurrent powers: Powers shared by the central government and the state governments, according to the specifications of the Constitution of the United States.

constitutional government: A government that is subject to limitations and that operates in accordance with general rules rather than arbitrarily. The existence of a constitution places a system of effective restraints on political power.

federalism: A form of government in which power is distributed between the central and regional units, each retaining sovereignty in specified spheres.

house rules committee: The group with the power to determine the specific time allotted for the debate of important legislation. This is one of the most important committees in the House of Representatives.

implied powers: Powers that are assumed by inference from the delegated powers granted to the central government, according to the Constitution of the United States.

judicial review: The power exercised by the Supreme Court to invalidate presidential, congressional, and state legislative action that it deems contrary to the Constitution of the United States.

Marbury vs. Madison: The case that established the principle of judicial review.

residual or reserved powers: Powers reserved for the states of the people, according to the Constitution of the United States.

rule of law: A constitutional principle holding that those in public authority derive, maintain, and exercise their powers on the basis of specific laws, and not on the basis of their personal power.

seniority rule: A principle strictly adhered to in Congress by which committee chairpersonships and memberships are determined by the years of service in Congress and on the particular committee.

separation of powers: An arrangement prescribed by the Constitution in which three separate branches of government are entrusted with the legislative, executive, and judicial functions.

HOW MUCH DO YOU RECALL? TEST YOUR KNOWLEDGE

MULTIPLE CHOICE QUESTIONS

1.   The system of distributing political power between a central national government and the governments of the geographical regions of the nation is called:
      a. confederacy
      b. federalism
      c. centralism
      d. unitarianism

2.   The chief reason that Congress is so ineffective is:
      a. that the Constitution delegates it so little power
      b. a result of the gradual emergence of the Supreme Court as a legislative body
      c. the development of the power of state governments
      d. the traditional organization of the legislative branch

3.   Which is not a restraint imposed on the United States government?
      a. Presidential supremacy
      b. Federalism
      c. Separation of power
      d. Checks and balances

4.   Which is not a presidential role?
      a. Chief Justice
      b. commander-in-chief of armed forces
      c. chief diplomat
      d. party leader

5.   Congressional representation is based on:
      a. single-member constituency system
      b. proportional representation
      c. parliamentary system
      d. only b and c

6.   Judicial review by the Supreme Court is based on:
      a. explicit statements in the Constitution
      b. the Marbury v. Madison decision
      c. an act of Congress
      d. the First Amendment to the Constitution

7.   The favorable evaluation of our presidents is based on:
      a. the caretaker role
      b. strict adherence to the written Constitution
      c. dynamic political leadership
      d. the teflon principle

8.   Congressional members in reality:
      a. represent local elites
      b. have little knowledge of what constituents want
      c. are interested in local welfare
      d. all of the above

9.   Some state powers are inferred from the powers specifically delegated by the
      Constitution to the central government. These are called:
      a. inferred powers
      b. residual powers
      c. implied powers
      d. reserved powers

10.   The federal system has worked particularly well in:
      a. large-sized countries with regional differences
      b. small, homogeneous countries
      c. small urban industrial countries
      d. large homogeneous single-religion countries

11.   The federal system is contrasted with a(n):
      a. unitary system
      b. confederate system
      c. catholic system
      d. none of the above
      e. **BOTH** unitary **and** confederate systems

12. Federalism may be defined as a system of:
    a. concurrent powers
    b. central power
    c. wholesale power
    d. regional power

13 The principle of separation of power had been discussed by the following political thinkers prior to their incorporation into the Constitution:
    a. Thomas Jefferson and Benjamin Franklin
    b. Adam Smith and John Maynard Keynes
    c. John Locke and Charles Montesquieu
    d. Alexis de Tocqueville and Jean-Jacques Rousseau

14. The President fills all but which of the following roles?
    a. Chief of state
    b. Speaker of the House
    c. Chief administrator
    d. Commander-in-chief of the Armed Forces

15. Which of the following is true?
    a. The president, Supreme Court Justices, and all members of Congress are elected by popular vote
    b. Senate members are elected but the members of the House are appointed by the president
    c. Each branch of government is brought to office by a different constituency
    d. Supreme Court Justices are appointed by the Senate and voted in by the House

16. When did the United States government begin to function as a cohesive unit?
    a. At the signing of the Declaration of Independence
    b. At the Constitutional Convention of 1787
    c. At the signing of the Articles of Confederation
    d. At the Inauguration of George Washington in 1789

17. What were the goals of the Constitutional Convention?
    a. To preserve the status quo
    b. To form a government that would serve the interests of all groups in the society
    c. To insure the power of the small farmers
    d. To diminish the power of a strong central government

CHAPTER 14

DEMOCRACY IN ACTION: WE, THE PEOPLE

In this chapter, you will learn

1. the differences among majoritarianism, pluralism and elitism;
2. which model of the location of political power best fits the United States;
3. the nature, functions, negative and positive facets of interest groups (including lobbies and PACs);
4. the nature, functions, purpose, weaknesses or strengths of political parties;
5. that voting is the chief form of political expression;
6. who does and does not vote in the United States;
7. some of the reasons for low voter turnout;
8. the meaning of public opinion;
9. the importance of the mass media in the political process.

TOPICAL OUTLINE

I. AMERICAN DEMOCRACY
II. HOW IS AMERICA GOVERNED
    A. Elitism
    B. Pluralism
        1. Conflict and Consensus
        2. A Realistic Democracy
III. INTEREST GROUPS
    A. Functions of Interest Groups
    B. Formation and Growth of Interest Groups
        1. Lobbyists
        2. PACs
    C. Shortcomings of Interest Groups
IV. POLITICAL PARTIES
    A. Purpose of Political Parties
    B. The Functions of Political Parties
    C. Features of the American Party System
    D. Winner Take All
    E. Third Parties
    F. The Party System in Decline
    G. Realignment or Dealignment?
    H. The High Cost of Campaigning

A. CHAPTER OVERVIEW

In the **classic conception of democracy**, individuals should be able to participate in the decisions of government directly. Participation is to be achieved through **majority rule**, but always respecting the **rights of minorities**. In a large and **heterogeneous** society, such direct participation is not possible. Yet, to make decisions binding on the entire society is to have the ultimate power to rule. If not the people, then who has this power in the United States? There are two **opposing schools of thought** on how power is distributed in this society.

According to **political pluralism**, or broker rule, power is diffused among numerous interest groups, and is not concentrated in a singly place. According to **elitism**, power is held by a limited number of individuals or groups. In reality, both views are probably correct, and the truth lies somewhere in the middle.

According to subscribers of both views, Americans are too apathetic, ill informed, and self interested to participate in the kind of system that democratic ideology prescribes. The **pluralists**, however, state that those in power are **responsive** to the people, even though the latter may be uninterested; so that while government is run by an elite, that elite is approved by the people. The **elitists** maintain that an apparent consensus is brought about by an elite which **manipulates** the masses through mass communication. **Public policy**, according to elitists, **reflects** not the demands of the masses, but the **values** of the elite.

There is disagreement also over the interplay of **conflict** and **consensus** in society, especially over which of the two predominates in the United States. Pluralists tend to belong to the consensus school of thought, according to which conflict takes place within a general framework of consensus. Elitists are likely to agree with the conflict school of thought, believing that ultimately, it is **force** that binds a society together. **Consensus is necessary for democracy** to work; but conflict keeps the system from stifling diversity and dissent. The right to **organize** an **opposition** for the purpose of gaining access to power in the process of decision making is a **fundamental element of democracy**. Such opposition usually takes the form of political **parties** whose primary purpose is to gain control of government and take on the responsibility for conducting its affairs.

Among the functions of political parties are: to **determine and define** the ideals and interests of the people, clarifying them as issues and ideologies; **to providing** the **personnel** necessary to run the government; to act as the loyal opposition (criticizing the party in power); and to educate the electorate in political matters. The American party system is a **two-party system**, and the two parties are not based on any particular doctrine or ideology. Rather, within each party there is a vast **variety of opinions** on specific issues and on how to achieve the goals of the society. American parties are **decentralized**, with diffused control. Finally, American parties are **durable**. Party organization consists of formal leadership, lower-echelon party activists, informal power holders (financial contributors), and passive voters. A frequent criticism of political parties is that their internal structure is undemocratic; but it is argued that as long as leaders remain responsive, internal democracy is unimportant.

What all agree should be reformed is the area of **campaign expenditures** and the time spent campaigning. Funds for electoral campaigns are provided by party activists who spend much time and energy on this activity although parties and their candidates depend on a few large donations from a small percentage of wealthy citizens. The Corrupt Practices Act prohibits any person from donating more than $5000 to any one political organization and forbids corporations, trade unions, and national banks to contribute. The law has produced an unintended side effect in the popularity of **Political Action Committees** (PACs) that have been so successful that more money has been poured into campaigns than ever before.

One can participate in political decision making by joining interest groups. **Interest groups** are **coalitions** of individuals with similar attitudes and interests who attempt to influence public policy.

179

Public policy is that which government does or does not do. Interest groups resemble political parties, but differ from them in the manner of pursuing their goals. The principal activity of interest groups is lobbying, or attempting to influence public officials into passing legislation beneficial to their members.

A. FILL IN THE BLANKS:

1. According to classical democracy, the power to make decisions binding on the society should belong to the_____.
2. Direct political participation is_____in a large and_____society.
3. There are two opposing schools of thought on how power is distributed in this society: _____and_____.
4. Power is diffused among numerous interest groups, according to the_____.
5. Power is concentrated in the hands of a limited number of individuals or groups, according to the_____.
6. A fundamental democratic right is to organize an_____.
7. In order for democracy to work, both _____and _____are necessary.
8. The primary purpose of political parties is to_____ _____ of government and take responsibility for_____its affairs.
9. Some of the functions of political parties include: _____and_____the interests of the people; providing_____to run the government; and acting as the _____ _____.
10. Characteristics of the American party system include: it is a_____ _____ _____; the parties are not based on a particular _____; and the parties are_____.

B. CHAPTER OVERVIEW

In studying voter behavior, social scientists have uncovered that there is a cynical **lack of faith** in democratic processes and in the right of some people to self government. In addition, democratic principles and values evoke a wide **consensus** when referred to in general terms, but not when the principles are applied to specific issues. There is also a **greater commitment** to democratic principles among the **leaders**, the politically active, well-educated elites **than among the masses** of people.

Although the United States was one of the first nations in the world to extend universal adult suffrage, only about 60 percent of its citizens vote in presidential elections. The **lowest voting record** occurs among unskilled workers with inadequate educations, and the **young**, the **underprivileged**, and **minority** groups. The reverse tends to be true of the college-educated, professional--managerial, and white-collar workers. The feeling among the politically alienated is that conventional political participation is meaningless. Gaps in information lead to contradictory opinions, and eventually to irrational voting.

Voting is acting on a political opinion. But the first amendment also guarantees each individual the right to have a **political opinion**. Public and political opinion are frequently used interchangeably, but they are not the same. Public opinion is the totality of opinions expressed by members of a community on any issue. **Political opinion** is the totality of opinions expressed by these same individuals on political issues alone.

Commentators in the communication media must select the events to be reported. This choice brings the public dangerously close to receiving propaganda instead of news, and to the selling of candidates and issues.

B. FILL IN THE BLANKS:

1. American voters appear to have a cynical_____of faith in the_____process.
2. There is consensus on democratic principles when they are presented in_____ _____.
3. There is greater commitment to democratic principles among the_____, the politically_____, and the_____ _____than among the masses.
4. Only about_____of the people vote in presidential elections.
5. The lowest voting record belongs to the_____, _____, _____, and _____.
6. Those who vote in greatest proportion tend to be_____ _____,_____ _____, and _____-_____workers.
7. The politically alienated believe that _____ _____ _____is meaningless.

8. The First Amendment guarantees Americans the right to hold a_____ _____.

9. Political opinion is the_____of opinions held by individuals on_____issues alone.

10. There is danger in the mass media of communication because commentators must_____what news to report, thus inviting_____.

TERMS TO REMEMBER

democratic pluralism: An interpretation of how the American political system works. This interpretation assumes that there are multiple centers of power, creating a situation in which political power is fragmented and diffused.

interest groups: Coalitions of individuals with similar interests who compete with one another for their share of political power, attempting to influence legislation in their favor.

lobbying: The principal activity of interest groups, consisting of attempts to influence public officials to pass legislation beneficial to the group or the people it represents.

majoritarian model of democracy: The classical model of democracy in which the statement "government by the people" is interpreted as meaning that the majority of the people make all government decisions directly.

party platform: A general statement of party positions and policies.

plural elites: Groups with diffused power and leadership roles, the representatives of different segments of the population to whom they are responsible through elections, interest groups, and partisan competition.

political opinion: The totality of opinions expressed by members of a community on political issues alone.

politics: The forces that make up and direct the government of the state, its policies, and its actions. Also, the institution that makes the decisions about "who gets what, when, and how" in society.

protest groups: Pressure groups characterized by protesting of certain governmental actions or inactions and calling attention to their grievances by such means as marches, sit-ins, demonstrations, and acts of civil disobedience.

public policy: That which government does or does not do.

ruling elite: A group composed of representatives of corporate, financial, military, and governmental interests who--according to some social scientists--make all the relevant decisions in the nation, irrespective of the wishes of the population at large.

HOW MUCH DO YOU RECALL? TEST YOUR KNOWLEDGE

MULTIPLE CHOICE QUESTIONS

1. One of the chief tenets of democratic ideology is that:
   a. popular participation must be representative
   b. the welfare of the community comes before the individual
   c. the individual has a major voice in public decisions
   d. the views of the minority have the same weight as those of the majority

2. Popular participation must be representative because:
   a. the size of the nation does not permit personal participation
   b. the ill and housebound cannot go to the polls
   c. not all people are acquainted with the issues
   d. many persons cannot pay the poll tax

3. The founders intended popular participation in government to be achieved through:
   a. the rule of elites
   b. majority rule with respect for rights of minorities
   c. rule by committee
   d. rule by minority coalitions

4.   What does it mean to govern?
     a. To govern is to have won the election for president.
     b. It is to have the power to make decisions binding on the whole society.
     c. To govern is to be in charge of the military.
     d. The idea of governing died with the monarchy.

5.   C. Wright Mills included in the political elite:
     a. the corporate rich
     b. the military upper echelon
     c. the political directorate
     d. all of the above

6.   According to pluralism, power:
     a. is held by one individual or a junta
     b. is concentrated in the hands of a few
     c. is diffused among numerous interest groups
     d. belongs to the people

7.   Elitism is a school of thought whose premise is that power:
     a. is diffused in society
     b. is held by the proletariat
     c. is limited to a few
     d. is shared only when issues are minor
     e. both c and d

8.   The basic purpose of political parties is to:
     a. provide the "loyal opposition"
     b. gain control of government and take on the responsibility for conducting its affairs
     c. represent the interests of the electorate
     d. build a platform

9.   "Realist democracy" states that:
     a. new social groups can become elites
     b. the elites present a consensus on basic democratic beliefs
     c. elites compete and rule through shifting coalitions
     d. all of the above

10. One of the criticisms of political parties is that:
    a. they tend to influence public policy
    b. they are unconstitutional
    c. their purpose is to seize power illegitimately
    d. their methods of campaigning involve too much time and expense

11. Which of the following is **not** true of PACs?
    a. PACs are created by presidential appointment
    b. PACs are established by interest groups
    c. PACs can donate money to any campaign they choose
    d. PACs are viewed by some as greater dangers than campaign contributors

12. Interest groups:
    a. address the overall interests of America
    b. represent the ideologies of their members
    c. have weakened the American party system
    d. are accountable to the voting public

13. The American party system is said to be in decline because:
    a. members of Congress vote straight party lines
    b. the Democratic party controls two branches of government
    c. voters split tickets and candidates run independently of their party's counsel
    d. PACs have replaced wealthy individuals as primary donors to individual candidates

14. The percentage of the American electorate that votes in local elections is:
    a. about the same as for the national elections
    b. around 10 percent
    c. about 50 percent
    d. less than 5 percent

15. The "free-rider" problem refers to:
    a. persons receiving free medical services for which they could afford to pay
    b. political patronage
    c. persons who refuse to join interest groups, but who still benefit from the successes of the interest group
    d. voters claiming to have voted for the winning candidate when they did not

CHAPTER 15

THE ECONOMY: CONCEPTS AND HISTORY

In this chapter, you will learn:

1. the purpose and functions of the economy as an institution;
2. the concepts that economists use in describing economies;
3. the historical development of Western economies;
4. the nature and features of the American economy in its historical framework;
5. the characteristics of the corporate hierarchy;
6. about the development, and some reasons for the decline, of the organized labor movement in the United States;
7. about the development of a global economic system and some reasons for the decline of American preeminence;
8. of the restructuring of the corporate bureaucracy and implementation of "lean" production methods, resulting in the revitalization of American productivity.

TOPICAL OUTLINE

I. THE ECONOMY AS AN INSTITUTION
    A. Economic Decision Making
    B. Basic Elements of the Economy
    C. Factors of Production
    D. Economic Choices and Opportunity Costs
    E. Limits to Output: Production Possibilities Frontier
    F. Specialization of Labor
    G. Trade, Barter, and Money
II. CONTEMPORARY ECONOMIC SYSTEMS: HOW CHOICES ARE MADE
III. WESTERN ECONOMIES IN HISTORICAL PERSPECTIVE
    A. The Birth of Capitalism
IV. ASPECTS OF INDUSTRIAL CAPITALISM
    A. The Corporate Form of Industrial Organization
    B. From Competition to Advertising
V. DIVERSIFICATION AND MULTINATIONALISM
VI. THE NATURE OF WORK IN THE INDUSTRIAL SOCIETY
    A. Shifting Sectors
    B. Professionalization

A. CHAPTER OVERVIEW

To sustain life, people need a constant supply of **food**, sufficient **shelter**, and **clothing** to protect them from extreme temperatures. These elements, unlike air or water that are also needed to survive, are **scarce** and require effort to obtain. The institution of the **economy** consists of those patterns of behavior that revolve around obtaining the scarce resources necessary for survival. The "economy," then, is an abstract concept representing **relationships** among people and groups of people who **behave** according to specific, traditional patterns in order to achieve the goal of survival.

In the face of the perpetual problem of scarcity of resources, each society must ask itself the following questions: **what should** be produced, and in what quantities? **how should** it be produced with the greatest efficiency? **for whom should** these commodities be produced? In short, decisions must be made about the **production, distribution and exchange**, and consumption of goods and services. These decisions are made differently in different societies. Some rely only on **custom and tradition**; others decide by the **command** of a ruler or body of representatives; others still reach these decisions as a result of the functioning of a **market system** dependent on supply and demand, prices, profits, and losses. Most modern economies use a variety of these methods of decision making. These decisions are analyzed within the context of **microeconomics**, an area of the discipline that is concerned with specific economic units and with the way in which such units function.

Additional economic decisions facing each society are: how to **utilize** fully a nation's resources? how to **keep constant** the purchasing power of money and savings? should production continue to **increase** or remain **stable**? The above decisions are studied in the context of **macroeconomics**, an area of the discipline concerned with the economy as a whole.

A. FILL IN THE BLANKS:

1. The basic problem facing people is that _____ needed for survival are _____.
2. In the face of scarcity, each society must decide: _____ to produce, _____ to produce it most efficiently, and ___ _____ it should be produced?
3. In different societies, these decisions are arrived at_____.
4. Some societies reach these decisions by relying on_____ and_____.
5. Other societies reach these decisions by the_____ of a ruler or ruling elite.
6. Still others use the _____ system dependent on_____ and_____, prices, profits, and losses.
7. The way in which these decisions are made are studied in the context of_____.
8. Societies must make additional_____ of an economic nature.
9. Societies must decide: how to_____ fully the nation's resources; how to keep the_____ _____ of money and savings stable; and whether the economy should_____ or_____ production.
10. These decisions are studied in the context of_____.

B. CHAPTER OVERVIEW

The goods and services that are produced in each society derive from the **resources** that exist naturally in that society, plus the **labor** of societal members. These natural resources are usually scarce and labor must be expended to accumulate them and utilize them. In economic terminology, resources are all those things that are **necessary for the production of goods and services**.

Thus, resources include **material things** (tools) and **human energy** (labor) used in producing goods and services.

Material things are either **natural** or **made by people**. The natural material things, called **land**, consist of land, minerals, and water. Material things made by people, called **capital**, consist of machinery, factories, shoes, pencils, etc. Together, labor, land, and capital are called **factors of production** because they are the basic elements that must be combined in the production of goods and services.

In addition to these basic factors, important elements in production are **technology, time, and efficiency**. Technology is the entire stock of **knowledge and skills** that a society possesses at any given time. **Time** is an economic resource that is scarce and precious. **Efficiency** is a way of obtaining the highest output of goods and services from a given combination of resources in the smallest amount of time. Resources are **versatile**: they can be put to different uses. But resources are also **finite**: they can be used up or destroyed, and cannot always be replaced. Resources and technology are the variables that affect the absolute **production possibilities** of society; but both resources and technology are fixed, so that production possibilities are ultimately **limited** (there is a limit to how much a society can produce).

Modern economies display such features as extreme **specialization** and division of labor, and they depend on **money** as the chief medium of exchange. Money is defined as a mechanism for facilitating barter. The **allocation** (distribution) of scarce resources is made differently in a market economy than in a command economy, although the two are just ideal models. Today, all economies are to some degree **mixed economies**, and the extent of the mixture and form that it takes are what determine whether an economic system is called **capitalistic, socialistic, or communistic**.

B. FILL IN THE BLANKS:

1. Resources include everything that is needed for_____
of goods and services.
2. Natural material things, called land, consist of_____,
_____, and_____.
3. Material things made by people, called capital, consist of
_____, _____, _____, etc.
4. The factors of production consist of _____, _____,
and_____.
5. Additional elements of production are_____,_____,
and_____.
6. Resources can be put to different uses: they are_____.
7. Resources can be used up or destroyed and cannot always be
replaced: they are_____.
8. Both resources and technology are fixed, so that production is
ultimately _____.
9. Some features of modern economies are:_____,
division of_____, and _____as a medium of
exchange.
10. Whether an economy is called capitalistic, socialistic, or
communistic depends on the degree and form of_____
between a _____and a_____system.

C. CHAPTER OVERVIEW

Industrialization made necessary not only the physical changes in
the **methods of production**, but also changes in **attitudes** and
values. Before the Industrial Revolution, artisans worked at home
and were paid for the raw material and labor. The profit motive
was unknown. With industrialization, not only did the **profit motive** become preeminent, but work became specialized, **machinery**
was used to speed it up, and workers and machinery were **housed
in the same place** for greater efficiency. By now, the industrial
system has long acquired specific patterns of organization. The
chief characteristic of this system is the invention of a form of
organization called the **corporation**.

The corporation is an enterprise **organized for large-scale
production**. To raise money, owners of an enterprise sell shares
of the company on the stock market. Buyers of the shares (shareholders) become co-owners of the new organization, or corporation. The corporation is **managed by executives** hired by a board

191

of directors who are elected by the stockholders. This separation of ownership from management was designed to minimize the profit motive and maximize the welfare of the corporation. The corporation is a **legal entity** that can acquire resources, own assets, manufacture and sell goods, extend credit or incur debts, sue and be sued, and perform similar functions **distinct** from its owners. The shareholders lose only their investment in case of bankruptcy, but are **liable for nothing** else. But what has made the corporation by far the most effective form of business organization is its ability to **raise capital** by pooling the savings of thousands of investors.

But there are problems with the corporation, too. First, many corporations have become **very large**, with practically a **monopoly of the market**, effectively squashing competition from smaller companies. This concentration of the productive wealth of the society in a few corporations is called **oligopoly**. Oligopoly is dangerous because lack of competition changes a free enterprise system into a monopoly; because financial power often translates into **political power**; because consumers are directed by **advertising** instead of competitive prices or quality; because of the **planned obsolescence** of products, ensuring ever greater consumption; and because of the **false needs** that are created only to supply consumers for the products. In addition, abuse occurs because many corporate executives and directors own controlling stock in the corporation, corporate directors of one company may be managers of another, and corporations own stock in other corporations.

New trends of corporations that lead to their ever greater size are **diversification and multinationalism**. Diversification is a corporation's acquisition of controlling shares in other corporations, often in totally different industries. Multinationalism is the habit of corporations to not merely export their products to foreign lands, but to **move** the production process into them, employing **cheaper local labor**.

C. FILL IN THE BLANKS:

1. Industrialization brought on physical changes in the_____ of production as well as changes in_____and _____.

2. The industrial system was more efficient because it brought_____and _____under the same roof, giving employers much more control.

3. The corporation is an enterprise organized for _____-_____ _____.

4. Shares of the corporation are sold on the _____ _____ and shareholders become _____.

5. The corporation is managed by_____hired by a_____ _____ _____voted in by the _____.

6. In a corporation, ownership is_____from management.

7. The corporation is a_____ _____capable of performing most economic functions apart from its_____.

8. The corporation is an effective business organization because of its ability to_____investors' money.

9. One of the problems with the corporation is the concentration of corporate power, or _____.

10. Some of the dangers in a concentration of productive power include: lack of _____, creating monopolies; financial power translating to _____power, advertising directing consumers instead of_____ or_____, and the interrelationships of_____.

D. CHAPTER OVERVIEW

For purposes of analysis the economy is divided into **three sectors**. The **primary sector** consists of the **extraction and processing of raw materials**, agriculture, fishing, mining, and forestry. The **secondary sector** is concerned with **manufacturing and building**, or turning raw materials into finished products. **The tertiary sector** represents the last stage of industrialization in which there is a great increase in **service** occupations.

With industrialization, there are dramatic **changes** in the sectors in which most workers are employed. In the early stages of industrialization (and before) the large majority of workers are employed in the primary sector. As industry progresses, the secondary sector shows a steady increase. The **tertiary sector** has had a tremendous spurt in growth from the beginning of the century, so that in this latest stage of industrialization the large **majority** of workers is employed in service occupations. This shift has resulted in important changes in the occupational structure because **more people** are becoming **professionals**, managers, or technicians, and there is **less need for unskilled or semiskilled occupations**. Such a transformation leads to changes in the stratification system of a society, causing chronic **unemployment** for that segment of the population that is unable to attain professionalization. **Professions** are not only specialized occupations, but occupations requiring **theoretical knowledge and training** in an art or a science. The attempts to professionalize have been successful among the white-collar workers of the tertiary sector, but not very successful in the first two sectors of the economy.

D. FILL IN THE BLANKS:

1. In order to study the economy, it is divided into_____.
2. Agriculture, mining, forestry, and extraction of raw materials belong in the_____ _____.
3. Manufacturing and building belong in the_____.
4. A large increase in service occupations occurs in the_____sector.
5. Industrialization brings about _____ _____in the_____ in which workers are employed.
6. In the early stages of industrialization, most workers are employed in the_____ sector.
7. In the latest stage of industrialization, most workers are employed in the_____ sector.
8. The occupational structure has undergone a shift as more people are becoming_____, _____, or_____.
9. There is less need for _____or_____workers.
10. Professions are_____occupations requiring _____knowledge and training.

E. CHAPTER OVERVIEW

Organization of labor in the United States began in 1880, when the AFL was reorganized and renamed and acquired a membership of four million of the five million unionized workers. The labor movement flourished again during the tenure of President **Roosevelt**, who **encouraged unionization** in the belief that it would give workers increased purchasing power, which in turn would **stimulate** the economy. The attempt to unionize **unskilled**

workers resulted in the creation of the **CIO**, which merged with the AFL in 1955. The first unions were **horizontal,** or **craft** unions, in which workers were divided according to their skills. Later came the **industrial or vertical** unions, in which workers were organized according to the industry in which they worked. The most important contribution of the labor movement to the welfare of workers has been **collective bargaining.**

Today, organized labor is experiencing growth pains, partly as a result of the decline of the secondary sector and the growth of the tertiary sector, whose workers have traditionally avoided unionization, and partly because of other factors. **American labor** is engaged in a **battle** with foreign labor, just as the American economy is challenged by sharp **competition** from Japan and Western Europe. It may be necessary to take steps to restore some **self-discipline,** as well as invest in **educating** the work force to prepare it for the twenty-first century.

E. FILL IN THE BLANKS:

1. The American labor movement originated in the last two decades of the_____century.
2. The labor movement began to flourish during the tenure of President _____.
3. President Franklin D. Roosevelt encouraged unionization because he thought it would give workers_____ _____-___.

4. Horizontal unions are structured according to individual _____.

5. Vertical unions include all workers employed in a specific_____.
6. Organized labor is experiencing a decline in membership partly as a result of the growth of the _____sector.
7. American labor is in competition with _____labor, particularly that of_____and_____ _____.
8. American labor needs to be _____and _____.

195

TERMS TO REMEMBER

capital: All material objects made by humans. One of the factors of production.

capitalism: An economic system in which property belongs to private individuals; production is engaged in for a profit motive; and prices, wages, and profits are regulated by supply and demand, as well as competition.   The welfare of the individual is the chief concern.

factors of production: Labor, land, capital, and entrepreneurship, or the basic elements that are combined in the production of goods and services.

finance capitalism: Capitalism associated with a later stage of industrialism in which business organizations are characterized by (1) dominance of investment banks and insurance companies, (2) large aggregates of capital, (3) ownership separate from management, (4) appearance of the holding company, and (5) appearance of the corporation.

industrial capitalism: Capitalism associated with an early stage of industrialism in which business organizations were mainly concerned with manufacturing, mining, and transportation.

labor: Human resources. One of the factors of production.

land: Natural material things such as land, minerals, water. Another of the factors of production.

monopoly: A situation in which one firm produces the entire market supply of a specific product.

multinational corporations: Corporations that extend production to foreign nations at great profit to themselves (because labor is cheap and markets are expanded) but at the risk of being perceived as threats to the hosts.

oligopoly: A condition of high industrial concentration in which a small number of corporations dominate an entire industry, effectively preventing price competition.

opportunity cost: The sacrifice involved in making an economic choice.

production possibility limits: The optimum amount of production that a society can attain. Each society faces a production-possibility frontier beyond which it cannot produce.

resources: Everything that is needed for the production of goods and services.

HOW MUCH DO YOU RECALL? TEST YOUR KNOWLEDGE

MULTIPLE CHOICE QUESTIONS

1. The primary function of the economy as a social institution is to:
   a. guarantee prosperity for all
   b. provide a blueprint showing people how to survive
   c. produce surpluses in all goods and services
   d. none of the above

2. Each society must make the following decisions of an economic nature regarding the:
   a. time, place, and quantity of production
   b. assessment, collection, and counting of taxes
   c. measurement of land, water, and minerals
   d. production, distribution, and consumption of goods and services

3. Resources are defined as:
   a. anything that is made by people
   b. anything that is produced in factories
   c. anything that is derived from natural ingredients
   d. everything that is needed for the production of goods and services including human energy

4. Land, labor, capital, and entrepreneurship are called:
   a. raw materials
   b. impetus to upward mobility
   c. factors of production
   d. external devices

5. A society's economic system is largely determined by its concept of:
   a. profit
   b. property
   c. surplus
   d. production

6. The following factors are important in production:
   a. technology
   b. time
   c. efficiency
   d. all of the above

7. The foremost advantage of a corporation is its:
   a. ability to accumulate vast amounts of capital in a short time
   b. capacity for protracted periods of employment
   c. ability to profit from the labor of its employees
   d. necessity to exhibit the latest technology

8. Professionalization means:
   a. excessive upward mobility
   b. interlocking directorates
   c. racial polarization
   d. none of the above

9. The economy, in relation to resources, deals with their:
   a. production
   b. distribution
   c. consumption
   d. none of the above
   e. all of the above

10. Which economic orientations govern Western industrial societies?
    a. Tradition
    b. Command
    c. Free Market
    d. both market and command

11. The production possibilities frontier refers to:
a. the amount of each commodity that can be produced given available resources
b. unlimited production of one commodity
c. limitless output of commodities
d. the fact that Third World nations do not allow their commodities to cross the borders into industrial societies.

12. When a few powerful corporations dominate an industry, the condition is called:
a. a free market for all
b. monopoly
c. oligopoly
d. government control

13. When Nabisco buys Domino Pizza, the process is called:
a. raiding
b. planned obsolescence
c. multinationalism
d. diversification

14. Unions today face some of the following problems:
a. the effects of the iron law of oligarchy
b. decline of heavy industry
c. loss of membership
d. all of the above
e. none of the above

15. Factors in the development of capitalism included:
a. the entrepreneurial spirit
b. wage labor
c. ownership of the factors of production
d. all of the above

CHAPTER 16

MICROECONOMICS AND MACROECONOMICS

In this chapter, you will learn

1. the difference between microeconomics and macroeconomics;
2. who the participants are in the market system;
3. what is the essence of the price system;
4. what are the market forces;
5. the need for a public sector and for government intervention in the economy;
6. about the economic goals of the society.

TOPICAL OUTLINE

I. THE SMALL PICTURE AND THE LARGE PICTURE
   A. Market Mechanisms
   B. Who Makes Decisions?
   C. Who Participates in the Economy?
   D. Markets
   E. Circular Flow
II. MARKET FORCES
   A. Demand, Supply, and Price
      1. Equilibrium
   B. The Principle of Laissez-Faire and Public Needs
III. A MACROVIEW
   A. The Public Interest: Socioeconomic Goals
      1. Full Employment
      2. Desirable Mix of Output
      3. High and Equitably Distributed Incomes
      4. Reasonable Price Stability
      5. Adequate Growth
IV. INSTRUMENTS OF PUBLIC POLICY
   A. Fiscal Policy
   B. The Function of Price and Employment Stabilizers
      1. Federal Budget
      2. Fiscal Decision Making
V. MONETARY POLICY
   A. Banks

B. Interest Rates
C. Regulating Banks
D. The Federal Reserve or the Fed

A. CHAPTER OVERVIEW

The **American** economy is a **mixed market economy** in which most workers are employed in the tertiary sector. In a market economy, decisions as to what is produced are basically made by **consumers** through a **price system**, meaning that the more consumers are willing to spend for a certain product, the more producers are willing to manufacture it. The participants in a market economy include: **households**, or those who live under one roof and make financial decisions as a unit; **firms**, or units that decide how to use labor, land, and capital (the factors of production) and which goods and services to produce; and **central authorities** that are all public agencies **government** bodies, and other organizations under the control of various levels of government.

In economic terminology, **markets** are **abstractions** referring to the demand for, the supply, and the price of a given product on a local or global level. **Product markets** are those in which firms sell their products; **factor or resource markets** are those in which households sell those factors of production which they control.

The **circular flow** is the process in which households earn money by selling their labor to firms, and firms, with that labor, produce goods and services which they sell to householders who pay for them with money earned with their labor. (Circular flow--from product markets to factor markets and back again.) The circular flow is **not** entirely a **closed** system because of withdrawals and injections. **Withdrawals** is income received by households that is not returned to firms, or income received by firms that is not returned to households. **Injections** is income received by firms that does not originate from the spending of households, and income received by households that does not originate from the spending of firms.

A. FILL IN THE BLANKS:

1. In a market economy, decisions as to what to produce are made
by_____through a _____system.
2. Participants in a market economy include:_____,
_____, and_____ _____.
3. Markets are _____representing _____,
_____, and_____on a local or global level.
4. Firms sell their products in_____markets; households sell their factors of production in_____or_____
markets.
5. Circular flow is the process in which factors of production flow
from_____ _____to _____ _____and
back again.
6. The circular flow is interrupted by_____and_____.

B. CHAPTER OVERVIEW

Market forces through which participants try to **maximize** their
happiness, profits, or the general welfare are **demand, supply,
and price**. Two basic exchanges take place in the market: energy
and labor flow in one direction, and money flows in the opposite
direction. **Supply** is what an individual gives up in an exchange.
Demand is what an individual obtains. Each participant in the
market is at some time both on the supply and on the demand side.
Demand is expressed as the individual's willingness and ability to
buy a specific number of products at a specific price. This is
graphically illustrated by a demand curve. Supply represents the
combined willingness of individuals or firms to supply specific
resources or products at specific prices; this is expressed by the
supply curve. The point at which supply and demand curves
intersect, meaning that the quantity supplied equals the price
buyers are willing to pay, is called **equilibrium**. Increasing or
decreasing purchases according to changes in price is called **price
elasticity**; demand is elastic when people buy more of a good in
response to a change in price, and inelastic when they buy little
even when the price is drastically cut.

The content and flow of goods and services, as well as prices at
which they are exchanged, are determined by the independent
actions of individual buyers and sellers without the intervention of
any central authority. This is called the *laissez-faire* doctrine, or
leaving things alone. The advantages of such a system include: it

allows people to feel free from constraint, to maximize each participant's goal, to use society's scarce resources in the production of
those goods and services for which there is greatest demand, and
to distribute goods and services on the basis of the amount of
purchasing power of each participant. Thus, the market system
answers **automatically** the three basic questions faced by every
economy. The disadvantages of the market system include the
fact that no provision is made for **public goods**, and that it works
to the advantage of those who already possess some resources,
thus **perpetuating inequality**. Those in control over a significant
proportion of productive resources are able to change market
outcomes in their own interest.

B. FILL IN THE BLANKS

1. Market forces that maximize participants' happiness, profits, or
general welfare include_____, _____, and_____.
2. The two basic exchanges that take place in the market are:
_____and_____flow in one direction, and_____flows
in the opposite direction.
3. Demand is what an individual_____in an exchange;
supply is what the individual _____ _____in an exchange.
4. One advantage of the market system is that it answers
_____the three questions faced by every society.

C. CHAPTER OVERVIEW

Because some of the results of the market system are not
consonant with the goals of the society, market economies have
had to accept a degree of **government intervention** in spite of the
laissez-faire doctrine. Although not easily defined, most would
agree that societal goals include: **full employment** (between 4 and
5 percent unemployment); a desirable **mix of output**; high and
equitably distributed incomes; reasonable **price stability**;
adequate growth--to produce enough goods and services for the
greatest number of people. Public policy is used to achieve some
of these goals: taxes and subsidies are used to redistribute unequal purchasing power; where there is no demand for a good or
service, yet there is a need for it; to counteract negative effects of
the economy, such as congestion, pollution, urban decay, etc;
controlling inflation; making sure that economic growth keeps up
with population growth; and ensuring that investments are stimu-
lated enough to increase productivity.

The government uses **fiscal actions**, **monetary** actions, and direct **regulation** to intervene in the economy. Fiscal policy is the use of **public expenditures** and **taxation powers** to change the outcomes of the economy. Taxes result in transferring buying power from the private to the public sector. By spending or not spending tax revenues, the government **affects** the level and mix of output, **redistributes** incomes, affects price stability and growth. **Fiscal** policy is known for its function as a **stabilizer**; it is a tool for achieving full employment and stable prices. When the government spends money, it **expands demand**, bringing full employment, resulting in higher consumption, further spurring demand, a process that is called the **multiplier effect**. **Inflation**, or excessive demand, is curbed by government action too: the government reduces its spending and raises taxes. As a result of its need to intervene in the economy, the Federal Budget is often out of balance, the government engaging in **deficit** spending and accumulating a huge public debt.

Monetary policy refers to the use of money and credit controls to affect economic outcomes. **Banks**, by extending or limiting credit, affect the money supply. By **raising or lowering interest rates**, banks can **stimulate** greater or lesser borrowing, affecting the amount of purchasing power in the circular flow. The ability of banks to extend credit is limited by the need to have the proper **reserve ratio**--the proportion of deposits that must be retained for withdrawal, transfer, and government regulation. The **Federal Reserve Bank** is the principal regulator of the money supply. It can establish minimum reserve requirements, it charges interest to lend to member banks, and it can buy and sell government securities, increasing or decreasing the amount of money in circulation.

C. FILL IN THE BLANKS:

1. Some of the goals our society aims for are:_____ _____, a desirable_____ __ _____, high and equal_____, reasonable_____ _____, and adequate_____.
2. Some of these goals are achieved through_____ such as_____and subsidies.
3. The government intervenes in the economy through_____ actions,_____ actions, and_____ regulation.
4. Fiscal policy is the use of_____and _____powers to affect the outcomes of the economy.

5. Taxes transfer _____ _____from the_____to
the_____sector.

6. By spending or failing to spend tax revenues, the govern-
ment_____the mix and level of output,_____incomes,
affects price and_____.

7. Fiscal policy is known in its function of_____.

8. Monetary policy refers to the use of_____and
_____controls to affect the outcomes of the economy.

TERMS TO REMEMBER

budget surplus: A surplus that occurs when the government's revenues are greater than its expenditures.

central authorities: All public agencies, generally referred to as "the government."

circular flow: Movement from product markets to resource markets and back again, that is interrupted by withdrawals and injections.

deficit spending: Spending that occurs when the government's expenditures are greater than its revenues.

discount rate: The interest rate charged by the Federal Reserve Bank for lending money to member banks.

discretionary spending: The portion of the federal budget that consists of current spending, rather than carryovers from previous years.

disposable income: National income less taxes and plus welfare payments. What people really have to spend or to save

equilibrium: The price and quantity at which both buyers and sellers are compatible--the quantity supplied equals the price buyers are willing to pay.

factor or resource markets: Markets in which households sell the factors of production that they control.

firms: Units that decide how to use labor, land, and capital and which goods and services to produce.

fiscal policy: The use of public expenditures and taxation powers by the government to change the outcomes of the economy.

full employment: A low rate of unemployment, between 4 and 5 percent.

GNP per capita: The total output of the economy divided by the total population.

Gross Domestic Product (GDP): The market value of all goods and services produced every year within the borders of a nation by residents and nonresidents alike.

Gross National Product (GNP): The total value in dollar-units of all goods and services produced in a nation during a given year.

household: All the people who live under one roof and who make financial decisions as a unit. Also called the consumer.

marginal productivity: The value people's work adds to total output.

market demand: The combined willingness of individuals and firms to buy a specific number of products at a specific price.

market supply: The combined willingness of individuals or firms to supply specific resources or products at specific prices.

monetary policy: The use of money and credit to control economic outcomes.

multiplier effect: Government spending that produces more income, results in higher consumption expenditures, and translates into a higher aggregate demand.

Net National Product (NNP): GNP less cost of depreciation for tools and machinery.

Phillips curve: A graphic illustration of the conflict between full employment and price stability: lower rates of unemployment are usually accompanied by higher rates of inflation.

product markets: Markets in which firms sell their production of goods and services.

uncontrollable expenditures: Expenditures from previous years built into the annual federal budget.

HOW MUCH DO YOU RECALL? TEST YOUR KNOWLEDGE

MULTIPLE CHOICE QUESTIONS

1. In a market economy, decisions about production are made by:
   a. command of ruling elite
   b. traditional forces in society
   c. a price system
   d. competing elites

2. Which of the following groups are involved in market transactions:
   a. households, firms, and central authorities
   b. consumers, producers, distributors
   c. wholesalers, shippers, workers
   d. advertisers, customers, retailers

3. A circular flow occurs from:
   a. demand to supply
   b. supply to demand
   c. banks to consumers
   d. product markets to factor markets and back

4. In a market economy, who gets the goods and services produced by firms?
   a. All members of society equally
   b. Only individuals involved in producing them
   c. Consumers who have the desire for them and the money to pay for them
   d. The strongest and smartest individuals in society

5. What are the goals of the participants in the mixed American economy?
   a. Consumers try to maximize their happiness
   b. Firms try to maximize their profits
   c. Government tries to maximize the general welfare
   d. All of the above

6. The two basic exchanges that take place in an economy are:
   a. energy and labor in one direction, and money in the other
   b. supply and demand
   c. wholesale and retail
   d. profit and deficit
   e. both a and b

7. When demand is inelastic, prices:
   a. go down
   b. go up
   c. stay the same
   d. equal costs

8. Demand is defined as:
   a. the circular manner in which market transactions occur
   b. an individual's willingness and ability to buy a specific product at a specific price
   c. what firms are willing and able to supply
   d. what government allows consumers to buy

9. Full employment really means:
   a. zero percent unemployment
   b. twenty to twenty-five percent unemployment
   c. four to five percent unemployment
   d. that all able-bodied persons can find work

10. An insufficient demand for, and an oversupply of, goods and services leads to falling prices and a condition known as:
    a. inflation
    b. deflation
    c. circular flow
    d. price elasticity of demand

11. An insufficient supply of goods and services and inability of demand to catch up leads to rising prices and a condition known as:
    a. inflation
    b. deflation
    c. supply and demand
    d. marginal productivity

12. When increased income results in greater spending and consequently a higher aggregate demand, the condition is called the:
    a. rippling effect
    b. Phillips curve
    c. multiplier effect
    d. inflationary spiral

13. The principal role of the Federal Reserve Bank is:
    a. chief regulator of the money supply
    b. to insure depositors against loss of deposits
    c. to lend money to individuals
    d. to borrow money from the federal government

14. When cars are offered at low prices but people still do not buy them, the situation is one in which:
    a. demand is elastic
    b. demand is inelastic
    c. there is aggregate demand
    d. exchange takes place

15. Some of the advantages of a market economy include:
    a. all participants get some satisfaction
    b. scarce resources are put into goods that are in demand
    c. economic output is available to those who can pay the price
    d. none of the above
    e. all of the above

16. When supply and demand are essentially equal, the economy is said to be in:
    a. a recession
    b. equilibrium
    c. equivalence
    d. abeyance

CHAPTER 17

GOVERNMENT AND THE ECONOMY: A MARRIAGE MADE IN HEAVEN?

In this chapter, you will learn

1. the contribution of John Maynard Keynes to economic theories;
2. the instruments at the government's disposal for intervening in the economy;
3. the reason for the imperfect functioning of these instruments;
4. the major economic problems faced by the economy, and how the American economy responds to them;
5. some of the instruments for evaluating the economy;
6. successes and failures of the American economy.

TOPICAL OUTLINE

I. INCOMES POLICY
    A. Economic Problems and Government Response
        1. Depression or Severe Recession
        2. Excessive Demand and Inflation
        3. Inflation and Unemployment
II. BUSINESS CYCLES
    A. Demand-Side Theories
    B. The Keynesian Revolution
        1. Monetarism
    C. Supply-side Theories
    D. Eclectic Theories
    E. Theory and Reality
III. EVALUATING THE PERFORMANCE OF THE ECONOMY
IV. THE AMERICAN ECONOMY: A SUMMATION
    A. Fitting Into the Global Economy

A. CHAPTER OVERVIEW

Incomes policy is a means of using **wage and price** controls to direct the economy. The policy is important when **inflation** and **unemployment** coexist. However, the policy changes the responsiveness of the market to demand and supply conditions, and it may lead to inequality of income distribution.

Specific problems for which government action is sought include: **depression** or severe **recession**; excessive **demand** and **inflation**; **inflation and unemployment**. Theoretically, the government should be able to respond to all economic problems, but in reality there are difficulties in **measurement** and **interpretation**.

There are a number of objective ways in which economists evaluate the performance of the economy. They measure the **GNP** (Gross National Product), which is the **total value in dollar units of all the goods and services produced in a nation in any given year**. More commonly, they are interested in the **GDP,** or the total output of goods and services produced within the limits of the United States, by American *or* foreign-supplied resources, as well as all income earned. Or they calculate the **per capita income** by dividing the national income by total population. They can also calculate the rate of economic growth by deducting the increase in GNP due to inflated prices or population increases.

A. FILL IN THE BLANKS:

1. Incomes policy uses_____and_____controls to affect the outcomes of the economy.
2. Government action is especially necessary in cases of _____,
_____, and_____.
3. The GNP is the total value, in dollar units, of all the_____
and_____produced in any given_____.
4. The per capita income is derived at by dividing _____
by _____ _____.
5. The true rate of economic growth can be found by deducting the increase in GNP due to_____ _____or _____ _____.

B. CHAPTER OVERVIEW

The United States disposes of a large number of natural resources. We have a large, healthy, and well-trained population, or human resources; and our capital resources are probably the largest in the world.

Nonetheless, many economists are now predicting that a profound **restructuring** of the economy is beginning to take place. First, there is change from an industrial to an **information** economy that involves a shift from a national economy to a **global** one. In practice, it means that the **smokestack industries** will be taken up by Third World countries, while the developed countries will concentrate on **high technology** and **information**. The strategic resource in an information society is **knowledge** and **data**; thus, it is thought that access to the economic system should be easier. In the interim, however, the transformation presents problems: decisions must be made as to what to do with the blue-collar segment of the work force and how to educate new generations to prepare them for the new economic order. Increasing **government** intervention seems to be in the cards, with the government becoming a **major employer**, as well as a regulator and coordinator of economic activities.

B. FILL IN THE BLANKS

1. The United States disposes of a large number of_____,
    _____, and _____resources.
2. Economists are predicting a profound_____of the _____.
3. The change from an industrial to an information economy involves a shift to
    a_____economy.
4. The smokestack industries will be taken up by the _____ _____ _____
    while the developed nations will concentrate on _____ _____
    and_____.
5. The most important resource in an information society is_____and_____.
6. Access to the economic system should be_____in an information society.
7. The role of government is fated to_____, with government becoming a
    major_____in the future.

Terms to Remember

budget surplus: A surplus that occurs when the government's revenues are greater than its expenditures.

deficit spending: Spending that occurs when the government's expenditures are greater than its revenues.

discount rate: The interest rate charged by the Federal Reserve Bank for lending money to member banks.

discretionary spending: The portion of the federal budget that consists of current spending, rather than carryovers from previous years.

disposable income: National income less taxes and plus welfare payments. What people really have to spend or to save.

fiscal policy: The use of public expenditures and taxation powers by the government to change the outcomes of the economy.

GNP per capita: The total output of the economy divided by the total population.

gross domestic product (GDP): The total output of goods and services produced within the limits of the United States, by American *or* foreign-supplied resources, as well as all income earned.

incomes policy: An attempt to use wage and price controls to direct economic outcomes.

inflation: A situation in which demand cannot be matched by an increase in supply, resulting in rising prices.

monetary policy: The use of money and credit to control economic outcomes.

multiplier effect: Government spending that produces more income, results in higher consumption expenditures, and translates into a higher aggregate demand.

net national product (NNP): GNP less cost of depreciation for tools and machinery.

Phillips curve: A graphic illustration of the conflict between full employment and price stability: lower rates of unemployment are usually accompanied by higher rates of inflation.

public sector: Economic activity on the part of the government in the name of the people or for the public interest.

social indicators: Ways of measuring the level of real welfare resulting from a specific level of output.

uncontrollable expenditures: Expenditures from previous years built into the annual federal budget.

HOW MUCH DO YOU RECALL? TEST YOUR KNOWLEDGE

MULTIPLE CHOICE QUESTIONS

1. During depressions or severe recessions, the government:
   a. increases expenditures
   b. cuts taxes
   c. prints paper money
   d. only a and b (cuts taxes and increases expenditures)

2. Market mechanisms:
   a. work to the advantage of those with existing resources
   b. advance social equality
   c. serve the interests of the majority
   d. provide for the production of public goods

214

3. A problem with *laissez-faire* economic policy is that there is:
   a. no flexibility
   b. no provision for public goods
   c. no profit motive
   d. responsiveness to demand

4. Adam Smith would approve of governmental support of:
   a. full employment
   b. protection of environment
   c. care for sick and needy
   d. none of the above
   e. all of the above

5. The problems encountered by the public sector include:
   a. difficulty in dismissing employees for incompetence
   b. small size of government agencies
   c. low expenditures
   d. none of the above
   e. all of the above

6. Inflation results when:
   a. demand exceeds supply
   b. supply exceeds demand
   c. there is control of purchasing power
   d. consumers have no purchasing power

7. The problem that arises when the government participates in the economy is that it:
   a. contributes to the training of skilled workers
   b. contributes to research and technology
   c. borrows large sums of money
   d. takes profits away from firms

8. The government can curb excessive aggregate demand (inflation) by:
   a. decreasing taxes on consumers
   b. increasing spending
   c. decreasing taxes on firms
   d. none of the above
   e. all of the above

9. When the government must pay for warships based on commitments made five years previously, the spending is called:
   a. discretionary
   b. uncontrollable
   c. balanced
   d. unavoidable

10. In order to deal with a situation of inflation and unemployment, the government must use:
    a. incomes policy
    b. antitrust action
    c. regular monetary and fiscal policies
    d. none of the above
    e. all of the above

11. The government's efforts at helping solve economic problems are hindered by difficulties in:
    a. measurement
    b. interpretation
    c. implementation
    d. none of the above
    e. all of the above

12. If the GNP increases by 8% and prices increase by 3%, the actual growth rate is:
    a. 11%
    b. 5%
    c. 8%
    d. 3%

13. In recent years, the income of the wealthy and affluent:
    a. remained unchanged
    b. decreased
    c. increased
    d. was redistributed to equalize the standard of living

14. In deciding to spend or not to spend tax revenues, the government:
    a. affects the level and mix of output
    b. redistributes incomes
    c. affects price stability and growth
    d. all of the above
    e. none of the above

15. Governmental action is used to solve all but which one of the following problems?
    a. Lack of competition in the public sector
    b. Depression or recession
    c. Excessive demand and inflation
    d. Unemployment and inflation

16. The American economy:
    a. has shown a great increase in the tertiary sector
    b. has shown an increase in professionalism
    c. has failed to protect consumers from greedy producers
    d. all of the above
    e. none of the above

CHAPTER 18

NATION AMONG NATIONS: INTERNATIONAL RELATIONS

In this chapter, you will learn

1. the definition of international relations;
2. theoretical perspectives from which scholars examine the international system;
3. additional levels from which the system can be viewed;
4. the participants in the international political system;
5. the objectives of states, as evidenced by foreign policy;
6. the means of attaining objectives, as measured by a state's use of diplomacy and other means;
7. the importance of the concept of power;
8. the meaning of "balance of power."

TOPICAL OUTLINE

I. THEORETICAL PERSPECTIVES ON INTERNATIONAL RELATIONS
    A. Realism
II. CONTEMPORARY PERSPECTIVES
    A. Pluralism
    B. Globalism
    C. Neorealism
III. PARTICIPANTS IN THE INTERNATIONAL SYSTEM
    A. Actors
IV. THE STATE AND THE NATION
    A. Classification of States
        1. Nonstate Actors
V. THE GOALS OF STATES
    A. The Competition of Objectives
VI. MEANS OF ACHIEVING GOALS: FOREIGN POLICY
    A. The Purpose of Foreign Policy
    B. Types of Foreign-Policy Decisions
IV. AMERICAN FOREIGN POLICY
    A. Goals
    B. The Role of Ideology

A. CHAPTER OVERVIEW

Interaction between and among states is the basic definition of **international relations**, a subdiscipline of political science. The discipline is analyzed from a variety of **theoretical** and **dimensional** levels that result in a multiplicity of conclusions. Most scholars agree that the most important participants in the international system are **states**, that states attempt to attain specific **objectives** by means of **foreign policies** and **diplomacy**, and that underlying the international system is **power** understood as **military strength**. Power in this context is defined as the capacity of a nation to use its tangible and intangible resources in such a way as to affect the behavior of other nations. The power of a nation is not always dependent on its capabilities. **National power** is influenced by both **psychological** and **relational factors**--how others view a nation and how powerful one nation is in relation to others.

Foreign policy is intended to **protect** and promote **national independence**, honor, **security**, and well-being. It is designed to pursue **national interest** as it is defined by each nation. Some political commentators believe that the pursuit of power is the central concern of national interest. Others suggest that national interest is determined by both **power and morality**. The goals that nations seek may be divided into those that are **competitive or absolute**, those that are **clearly** defined or diffuse, those that are **declaratory** or **action-oriented**, and those that are **static** or **dynamic**. The nature of national interest is not explained by single-factor concepts.

A. FILL IN THE BLANKS:

1. Interaction between and among states is the basic definition of

_____ _____.

2. The discipline is analyzed from a number of theoretical and dimensional levels resulting in a multiplicity of_____.

3. Underlying the international system is _____ understood as _____ _____.

4. In this context, power is defined as the _____ of a nation to use its tangible and intangible resources in such a way as to_____the behavior of other nations.

5. Foreign policy is intended to protect and promote national

_____, _____, and _____-_____.

6. The goals that nations seek include those that are_____ or _____, clearly defined or_____, declaratory or_____, static or_____.

B. CHAPTER OVERVIEW

Foreign policy is made by **individuals** who are pressured and influenced by others, by psychological factors, and by specific conditions and are limited by the organizational context in which they operate. There are **three types** of foreign policy decisions: (1) **general** foreign-policy decisions, expressed in policy statements and direct actions; (2) **administrative** decisions made by the governmental bureaucracy; and (3) **crisis** decisions made when one state feels that a specific situation marks a turning point in its relationships with one or more other states.

Foreign policy is affected by domestic policy. American domestic policy is guided by the **democratic ideology**, including revolutionary ideals and the concept of freedom. Although Americans do not always act according to this ideology, they are officially committed to it. The problematic aspect of foreign policy is that other nations subscribe to other ideologies, some of which **conflict** with the American ideology.

In the course of American foreign policy, the country has been **isolationist, interventionist, internationalist**, and a supporter of the **containment** policy, or rabidly anticommunist. This last policy led the United States into the unpopular and costly Vietnam War. In the 1970s, American foreign policy was characterized by the spirit of **detente**.

B. FILL IN THE BLANKS

1. Foreign policy is made by _____, _____
   _____, and _____ _____.
2. Foreign policy decisions may be_____,_____,
   and _____.
3. American domestic policy is guided by the_____
   _____.
4. In the course of American foreign policy, the nation has been
   _____, _____, and a
   supporter of the containment policy.

C. CHAPTER OVERVIEW.

The analysis of foreign policy should include questions regarding nation's **values, roles, and instruments**. The values of American foreign policy changed from a **defense of democracy** to rabid **anticommunism**, and are in the process of changing toward peaceful **coexistence**. The instruments of foreign policy, or tools with which something is accomplished in the international arena by manipulating nations, include: the **United Nations**, foreign **aid**, **collective security, the military establishment**, and **propaganda**.

The United Nations is not powerful enough because most decisions that affect world peace are made by the governments of the major powers. American aid to nations around the world has probably helped contain communism, and has also helped the

222

economies of various nations. **Treaties and security arrange-ments** improve relations between and among nations, but they are never really totally dependable.

Although the United States professes to want to **halt** the production of arms, weapons production and stockpiling continue to **escalate**, although there are some signs that the arms race is abating. The arms race spirals because each power must keep up with the technology of other powers if possession of nuclear arms is to act as a deterrent to mutual destruction. Propaganda--an ideology that someone tries to spread to convince others of its rightness--sometimes leads us to stretch the truth or to direct it at our own citizens. Many government agencies and departments are engaged in propaganda.

C. FILL IN THE BLANKS:

1. Foreign-policy analysis includes _____,
_____, and _____.
2. Instruments of foreign policy are the_____ _____,
_____ ____, _____ _____, the military,
and propaganda.
3. The United Nations is not powerful enough because most decisions are made by the_____of the major powers.
4. Treaties and security arrangements are never really
totally_____.
5. Propaganda sometimes leads us to_____the truth.

D. CHAPTER OVERVIEW

Morality has always been considered a necessity in foreign policy, at least on the part of the "civilized" world. But it is **difficult to define** morality, which is relative to time and circumstances. It appears that for now it is necessary to settle for morality in the form of rhetoric rather than as a prescription for actual behavior.

Diplomacy is the conduct of international relations by **negotiation**. Its purpose is the pursuit of national goals without offending any nation. Diplomacy is an old procedure, although it has changed in character in this century. The power of diplomacy is **limited** because there are fundamental differences among the major powers and because diplomats in democratic countries are unsure of their roles.

A **balance of power** was maintained for several hundred years after the creation of nation-states by a **system of shifting alliances** that ensured that **no single state** or coalition would become **stronger** than any other. This **multipolar** balance of power began to decline at the turn of the century, a bipolar system--with the United States and the Soviet Union as its poles--took its place following World War II. Today, the balance of power is again shifting, but it is not clear in what direction.

D. FILL IN THE BLANKS

1. Morality is_____to time and circumstances.
2. The conduct of international relations by negotiation is the definition of_____.
3. The power of diplomacy is_____because there are fundamental_____among the major powers.
4. A balance of power was maintained for several centuries by a system of _____ _____.
5. The balance of power ensured that no single state or coalition would _____ _____than the others.
6. The _____balance of power began to decline at the turn of the century, and a _____system took its place.

TERMS TO REMEMBER

administrative foreign policy: Decisions made by the government bureaucracy.

containment: American foreign policy in the period following World War II, attempting to contain what were perceived as the imperialist goals of the Soviet Union.

crisis foreign policy: Urgent decisions made when one state feels that a situation will mark a turning point in its relationship with another state. Crisis decisions are a combination of general and administrative decisions.

detente: Foreign policy dependent on peaceful negotiations rather than containment.

diplomacy: The conduct of international relations by negotiation.

foreign policy: Goals intended to protect and promote national independence, national honor, national security, and national well being.

general foreign policy: Decisions expressed in policy statements and direct actions.

internationalism: American foreign policy in the late 1930s and during World War II, in which there was a commitment to principles of nonaggression and self-determination.

interventionism: American foreign policy of the early twentieth century, in which the United States intervened militarily in other nation-states to "make the world safe for democracy."

isolationism: Early American foreign policy of staying clear of permanent or entangling relationships and alliances with other nation states.

Truman doctrine: Foreign policy giving the support of the United States to free nations so that they could maintain their free institutions and national integrity against the imposition of totalitarian regimes.

HOW MUCH DO YOU RECALL? TEST YOUR KNOWLEDGE

MULTIPLE CHOICE QUESTIONS

1. "The capacity of a nation to use its resources to affect the behavior of other nations" is a definition of:
    a. foreign policy
    b. diplomacy
    c. power in the context of international relations
    d. international law

2. Foreign policy decisions may be categorized into those that are:
   a. general
   b. administrative
   c. crisis
   d. all of the above
   e. none of the above

3. Among the goals of United States foreign policy are the protection of:
   a. the nation's physical security
   b. the security of our main allies
   c. the economic security of the nation
   d. all of the above
   e. none of the above

4. The oldest goal of American foreign policy, articulated by the Monroe Doctrine, was to:
   a. develop friendly ties with the Soviet Union
   b. keep peace in the Middle East
   c. keep foreign powers out of North and South America
   d. be the first atomic power

5. Realism posits that:
   a. the state is a rational actor in international relations
   b. economics and culture are central to politics
   c. foreign policy is often self-contradictory
   d. the essence of politics is the pursuit of wealth

6. "Gunboat Diplomacy" was used in which stage of American foreign policy?
   a. Isolationaism
   b. Containment
   c. Interventionism
   d. The Cold War

7. The term "detente" has been used to denote a kind of foreign policy based on:
   a. aggressiveness
   b. containment
   c. peaceful negotiations
   d. hiding behind an iron curtain

8. What should an analysis of foreign policy include?
   a. Values
   b. Roles
   c. Instruments
   d. All of the above
   e. None of the above

9. The view that the U.S. ought to remain involved in the international community by means of providing foreign aid, arms control, and U.N. peacekeeping efforts is called:
   a. isolationism
   b. cooperative internationalism
   c. interventionism
   d. *laissez-faire* containment

10. The military-industrial complex depends on:
    a. huge defense spending
    b. a large bureaucracy
    c. research in military technology
    d. all of the above
    e. none of the above

11. American propaganda:
    a. delivers America's message to the world
    b. involves several government agencies
    c. sometimes distorts the truth
    d. none of the above
    e. all of the above

12. Diplomacy today gives diplomats:
    a. great discretion in making policy decisions
    b. limited roles as messengers
    c. charge of summit conferences
    d. starring roles as celebrities

13. Neorealism maintains that states face three problems:
    a. other states, elites, and classes
    b. anarchy, order, and constraints
    c. war, revolution, and famine
    d. the military, intellectuals, and bureaucrats

14. Globalists view international relations:
    a. from a historical perspective
    b. as taking place within a world capitalist system
    c. in terms of dependency relations
    d. all of the above

15. IGOs are:
    a. transnational organizations which bypass government
    b. multinational corporations
    c. voluntary associations of foreign states
    d. national liberation and terrorist groups

CHAPTER 1

ANSWERS TO FILL IN THE BLANKS:

A. I. social universe
    2. objectivity
    3. objective, emotional
    4. relationships
    5. physical sciences

B. I. hypothesis
    2. Empirical research
    3. classification and organization

C. I. anthropology
    2. Archaeology
    3. sociology
    4. psychology
    5. economics
    6. political science
    7. social science

D. I. statistical correlation
    2. probability statistics
    3. sampling techniques
    4. judgment

ANSWERS TO MULTIPLE CHOICE QUESTIONS

1. c	2. d	3. d	4. a	5. c
6. a	7. c	8. d	9. b	10. a
11. d	12. b	13. d	14. c	15. c

CHAPTER 2

ANSWERS TO FILL IN THE BLANKS:

A. I. 8, 12 billion

2. gravity
3. expand
4. dark matter
5. 2 billion
6. hotter, melt
7. one-celled microorganisms
8. animals

B. I. changeable
    2. hierarchy
    3. I9th
    4. extinct
    5. Charles Darwin
    6. natural selection
    7. extinct
    8. disappear
    9. dominant, recessive

C. I. genetics
    2. genes
    3. blueprint
    4. chromosomes
    5. 46, nucleus
    6. 23
    7. genotype
    8. visible, external
    9. DNA
    I0. mutation, genetic drift, gene flow, and speciation
    II. speciation
    I2. isolated

D. I. heredity
    2. race
    3. limited gene pool
    4. physical, social
    5. expansionism
    6. adaptation
    7. classified
    8. Negroid, Mongoloid, Caucasoid
    9. biochemical factors
    10. hybrids, between

E. 1. animals

2. adapt
3. 225
4. mammals
5. grasping mechanism, vision, cerebral cortex
6. monkeys, apes
7. side by side
8. <u>Homo sapiens</u>
9. <u>Cro-Magnon</u>
10. Fertile Crescent, Near East

F.   I. social
2. males
3. cooperation, sharing, incest taboos
4. organization
5. fire

ANSWERS TO MULTIPLE CHOICE QUESTIONS

I. d	2. b	3. d	4. a	5. a
6. b	7. d	8. b	9. d	10. d
11. a	12. b	13. d	14. b	15. d

CHAPTER 3

ANSWERS TO FILL IN THE BLANKS:

A.   I. biological makeup
2. grasping, holding, manipulating
3. judge distances, three-dimensionally
4. brain
5. think abstractly, remember, symbolize
6. communicate
7. weakness, instincts

B.   I. social interaction
2. knowledge, values, ideas, goals
3. socialization
4. socialization
5. patterns or systems, behavior
6. culture
7. signals, genetically transmitted

231

8. language, gestures, music
9. transmitted, created
10. reality

C.   I. material and nonmaterial
2. material culture
3. nonmaterial culture
4. normative
5. values, norms, institutions, sanctions
6. values
7. norms
8. folkways, mores, taboos, and laws
9. norms
I0. conform
II. sanctions
I2. belong

D.   I. trait
2. culture complex
3. institution
4. pressing human needs
5. family
6. pivotal

E.   I. ethnocentrism
2. cultural relativity
3. universal norms, moral absolutes
4. cultural universals
5. diffusion
6. invention, discovery, planning
7. time to adjust

F.   I. within
2. heterogeneous
3. subculture
4. race, religion, nationality, occupation
5. inferiority
6. counterculture

ANSWERS TO MULTIPLE CHOICE QUESTIONS:

I. c   2. b   3. b   4. a   5. c

6. d	7. d	8. a	9. d	10. b
11. c	12. d	13. b	14. d	15. d

CHAPTER 4

ANSWERS TO FILL IN THE BLANKS:

A.
    I. communication
    2. symbolic interaction
    3. social relationships
    4. patterns, social system
    5. structure and organization
    6. statuses, roles
    7. status
    8. status, does
    9. ascribed
    10. achieved
    II. multiplicity, roles
    12. master
    13. role confusion, conflict (stress)

B.
    I. group
    2. symbolic interaction, group membership, values, rules, and goals.
    3. size
    4. dyads, triads, family and friendship groups
    5. in and out, reference, voluntary and involuntary
    6. primary and secondary
    7. primary
    8. secondary
    9. Secondary, primary

C.
    I. society
    2. social system
    3. social relationships
    4. nation state
    5. social organization, mode of substistence
    6. hunting and gathering, pastoral, horticultural, agrarian, modern industrial
    7. urbanization, mechanization, bureaucratization
    8. social organization
    9. Gemeinschaft, Gesellschaft
    10. small size, little division of labor, primary relationships

(family focal unit, customs and traditions important, homogeneity, integrated social unit.)

II. large size, complex division of labor, social institutions (agencies, secondary relationships, heterogeneity.)

D.   I. interacting
2. symbolic
3. words, gestures
4. social processes
5. cooperation, competition, conflict
6. order
7. Society
8. social organization
9. individual freedom
I0. roles

F.   1. formal organizations
2. groups, achieving a goal
3. bureaucracy
4. formal structure, relative permanence, hierarchy of roles, a formal program
5. large-scale formal organizations
6. hierarchical, rationally, labor, authority
7. specialization, hierarchy, rules, impersonality, merit, job tenure
8. change, rules, size and influence
9. dynamism, informality
I0. unwilling, leadership

ANSWERS TO MULTIPLE CHOICE QUESTIONS

I. c	2. d	3. c	4. b	5. a
6. d	7. d	8. d	9. b	10. a
11. d	12. c	13. c	14. d	15. d

CHAPTER 5

ANSWERS TO FILL IN THE BLANKS:

A.   I. behavior, thought, emotions
2. attitudes, values, beliefs, habits, goals, and actions
3. dynamic, unique

4. affects and is affected by
5. distinctive
6. need for care, for love, and lack of instincts
7. socialization
8. transmission

B. I. biological organism, human being
    2. other people
    3. fundamentals, skills, aims, roles
    4. identity
    5. family

C. I. socialization, psychodynamic theories
    2. Charles Horton Cooley
    3. symbolic interaction
    4. biological drives
    5. Sigmund Freud
    6. unconscious processes, dream, psychoanalysis
    7. oral, anal, phallic, latency, genital
    8. learning, conditioning
    9. stages, physical maturation
    I0. family, school, peer group, mass media
    11. self-actualization

D. 1. ongoing, statuses, roles
    2. resocialization
    3. life cycle
    4. total institutions
    5. resocialization

E. 1. socialization, temperament, disorders
    2. negatively perceived
    3. relative
    4. permissibile behavior, function
    5. social change
    6. genetically
    7. mental defects, abnormality, illness
    8. psychosomatic
    9. anxiety reaction, phobias, depression
    10. Sociopaths
    11. schizophrenia, paranoia, manic depression
    13. Robert Merton's

14. learning theory
15. labeling
16. self-actualization
17. improve

ANSWERS TO MULTIPLE CHOICE QUESTIONS:

I.	c	2.	b	3.	a	4.	d	5.	c
6.	d	7.	b	8.	d	9.	b	10.	b
11.	d	12.	d	13.	c	14.	d	15.	a
16.	c	17.	a	18.	a	19.	b	20.	c

CHAPTER 6

ANSWERS TO FILL IN THE BLANKS:

A.
1. social
2. differentiates
3. social class, gender, race and ethnicity, age
4. genetic traits, levels of intelligence, social class
5. complex and affluent
6. rank themselves
7. wealth, prestige, power

B.
I. unavoidable
2. law of nature, selfishness and greed
3. liberal
4. society, individual
5. system of rewards
6. conflict and dissension
7. social change
8. Karl Marx
9. one class, interest
I0. classless

C.
1. scarce, prized
2. class, status, power
3. power, privilege, prestige
4. ranked, social system
5. occupation, source of income, color, education, sex, age, religion, ethnic origin

6. control, consent
7. personal, social
8. potential
9. stratification system

D.   I. wealth, power, prestige
      2. caste, estate
      3. SES index
      4. 2,3
      5. lower upper
      6. one-half, upper, middle, lower
      7. globalization, layoffs, unemployment
      8. 15, poverty line, average
      9. relative, absolute
      10. homeless, underclass, new, overclass
      11. child rearing, education, values

E.   1. move up or down
      2. American dream
      3. movement, down, up, down
      4 education
      5. special talent
      6. insignificant

F.   1. dramatic, world poverty
      2. 77, 5.5
      3. hunger, housing, disease
      4. inequality
      5. reallocation, technological
      6. transition, industrial, informational
      7. minority, stratified

ANSWERS TO MULTIPLE CHOICE QUESTIONS:

I. b	2. d	3. c	4. a	5. b
6. b	7. a	8. a	9. c	10. d
11. d	12. a	13. c	14. b	15. c
16. d				

CHAPTER 7

ANSWERS TO FILL IN THE BLANKS:

A. 1. race, ethnicity, religion
    2. category, power, prestige, privilege
    3. minorities, wars, migrations
    4. biological, cultural
    5. subordinate, sticking, within the group, descent
    6. minorities
    7. Anglo-conformity
    8. Americanized
    9. melting-pot ideology
    10. New American
    11. fuse, biologically, culturally
    12. religion
    13. cultural pluralism
    14. pluralism, assimilation, acculturation, accommodation.
    15. amalgamated
    16. value system, behavioral norms
    17. institutionalizes
    18. genocide

B. 1. biological
    2. transmitted
    3. stereotyping
    4. entire, individual
    5. cultural distinctiveness
    6. prejudice, discrimination
    7. having all the facts
    8. acting
    9. learned, insecurity, social isolation, emotionally satisfying
    10. attitudinal, institutional

C. 1. blacks, involuntarily
    2. slavery, cultural ties
    3. underclass
    4. community, language, religion
    5. urban skills, commitment
    6. native Americans, tribal, receptive
    7. l9th, gold, railroads
    8. yellow peril, hard work, frugality, education

9. Asians, upward mobility
10. other ethnic
11. one

D. I. infancy
    2. three
    3. conditioning, imitation, self-definition
    4. anatomical, genetic, hormonal
    5. verbal ability, spatial and quantitative
    6. aggressive, nurturant
    7. inequality
    8. options
    9. sociocultural change
    10. unclear

E. 1. social, biological
    2. highly valued
    3. socially-invented
    4. knowledgeable
    5. ageism
    6. diminished, productive
    7. health care, depression

ANSWERS TO MULTIPLE CHOICE QUESTIONS

I. b	2. c	3. c	4. d	5. d
6. b	7. d	8. b	9. d	10. c
11. c	12. d	13. b	14. b	15. c
16. c	17. d	18. d	19. d	20. c
21. b	22. a	23. c	24. b	25. a
26. c	27. b	28. b	29. d	30. c
31. c				

CHAPTER 8

ANSWERS TO FILL IN THE BLANKS:

A. 1. change
    2. statics, dynamic
    3. technology
    4. physical, mental
    5. standard of living, diseases, life

6. urbanization
7. organization, bureaucracy
8. rising expectations
9. sexual standards (norms), as well as the attendant roles
10. weapons

B. 1. change
2. preindustrial, industrial, all areas
3. postindustrial
4. system of production, subsistence
5. traditions, way of life
6. cities, industrial, wages, secondary, nuclear
7. values, systems, personalities
8. integration
9. dislocation, strain, rootlessness, anomie
10. unstable

C. 1. methods, devices, artifacts, control
2. agricultural
3. population growth, permanent settlements, institution-building
4. cities, labor, trade
5. 1750s, materials, sources of power
6. mechanization, power, factory, transportation, communication
7. second, computer age
8. production, divided, steps
9. control
10. material, social problems, disorganization

D. 1. guessed
2. contemporaneously, culture
3. interaction, new statuses, roles
4. values, norms, beliefs, material objects
5. innovation, discovery, invention, diffusion
6. elements, cumulative
7. planning, reform, revolution
8. perception
9. existing, use
10. physical environment, size, special individuals, events

E. 1. mass society
2. social disorganization, integrated
3. distributed, anonymous
4. continuum, Gesellschaft

5. primary, secondary
6. high mobility, anonymity, roles and statuses, integrative
7. led, elite
8. collective behavior, violent
9. reached

ANSWERS TO MULTIPLE CHOICE QUESTIONS

1. c	2. c	3. a	4. c	5. b
6. c	7. b	8. c	9. d	10. d
11. c	12. d	13. d	14. a	15. c

CHAPTER 9

ANSWERS TO FILL IN THE BLANKS:

A.   1. standard of living, Industrial Revolution
2. birthrates, death rates, sex ratios, age groups, marriage and divorce incidence, and human mobility
3. density
4. births, 1,000, year
5. high

B.   1. 35
2. arithmetic
3. Western, high
4. Zero population growth

C.   1. cultural, technical
2. size, age, sex
3. population pyramid
4. median age, three

D.   I. Urbanization
2. suburbanization
3. lower death rates, higher birthrates, immigration
4. 2500
5. condition, attitudes, way of life
6. rural, primary relationships, historical continuity, emotional involvement
7. suburbanization
8. SMSAs, megalopolis (urban sprawl)

9. slums, ghettos, opportunity
10. Gentrification, urban renewal

E. 1. natural conditions, resources
2. land forms, climate, vegetation, soils, animals, waters, and minerals
3. reciprocal, people
4. simple, direct
5. perceived, exploited
6. high population density
7. people
8. overpopulation, population density

F. 1. interact, interrelate
2. balance, continue
3. local, regional, global
4. environmental pollution, environmental depletion, overpopulation
5. tampering, damaging
6. burning, fossil fuels
7. air pollution
8. water pollution
9. resource depletion
10. EPA, business community

ANSWERS TO MULTIPLE CHOICE QUESTIONS:

I. c	2. d	3. b	4. a	5. d
6. b	7. a	8. d	9. d	10. b
11. b	12. c	13. b	14. c	15. b
16. b	17. d	18. b	19. a	20. d
21. b	22. b	23. c		

CHAPTER 10

A. I. clear-cut, normative system
2. spontaneous, unpredictable, unstructured, unplanned
3. rapid social change
4. temporary, stimulus
5. casual, organized, expressive, acting
6. common mood, identity, norms
7. guilt, do, target
8. rumors, fads, fashions, crazes, publics, public opinion
9. LeBon

10. Herbert Blumer
11. contagion, convergence, emergent norm

B. 1. collection, share, affected
    2. intellect
    3. temporary, dispersed, composition
    4. complex (heterogeneous), traditional
    5. public opinion
    6. public opinion
    7. traditional, conflicting
    8. propaganda, censorship
    9. one-sided
    10. deletes

C. 1. forms, altering
    2. ideologies
    3. ideologies
    4. explanation, reinforcement, direction
    5. institutionalized
    6. long-lived, large numbers, directed
    7. social change, alienation (normlessness), deprivation, expectations
    8. reform, revolutionary
    9. nationalistic, class
    10. change resistant

ANSWERS TO MULTIPLE CHOICE QUESTIONS

1. b	2. b	3. c	4. b	5. c	6. c
7. c	8. c	9. a	10. b	11. d	12. a
13. c	14. b	15. a	16, b	17. c	18. c
19. d	20. d				

CHAPTER 11

ANSWERS TO FILL IN THE BLANKS:

A. 1. systems, rational, intelligible, logical
    2. sets of attitudes
    3. picture, should be
    4. times of crisis, dominant, unacceptable
    5. comprehensive, abstract, reductionist

6. justification to government, structure, mission and purpose
7. who will govern, selected, principles
8. persuade, opposing
9. retaining, reforming, abolishing
10. monolithic, socialized, conflicting

B.   1. person, group, power
       2. right, left, totalitarian
       3. revolt, better, in all spheres
       4. single, kept alive, interprets
       5. fascism, Italy, 1922, nazism, Germany
       6. distrust, basic equality, violence
       7. capital, labor, state

C.   1. value, free, moral, rational, rights
       2. people's consent
       3. trustee, assigned
       4. subideology, political, economic
       5. Adam Smith, *The Wealth of Nations*, 1776
       6. private property, profit, free, competition
       7. mixed, intervention, competition, failure
       8. equal opportunity
       9. political, economic
     10. state, government
     11. property

ANSWERS TO MULTIPLE CHOICE QUESTIONS:

1. d	2. b	3. a	4. c	5. d	6. c	7. a
8. a	9. d	10. d	11. c	12. b	13. a	14. d
15. c	16. b	17. a	18. c			

CHAPTER 12

ANSWERS TO FILL IN THE BLANKS:

A.   1. social order
       2. group, social control
       3. power
       4. social control

5. institutionalized
6. power
7. moral control
8. political control
9. when, how, whom
10. protects, maintains, regulates

B.
1. power
2. in spite of resistance
3. rewards, coercion, influence
4. state, government
5. authority
6. legitimate
7. right and proper
8. authority
9. coercion
10. traditional, legal-rational, charismatic

C.
1. process, group of people
2. abstract, symbol
3. permanent, temporary
4. population, territory, government, sovereignty
5. Thomas Hobbes, John Locke
6. social contract, state of nature
7. protection, social order
8. reason, social, reasonable
9. limited, consent, protection
10. functionalism, conflict

D.
1. clans, tribes, city-states, nation-states
2. abstract, culture group, political state
3. nationhood
4. geographic boundaries, commercial ties, language, history, literature, future
5. supreme authority, impermeable and impenetrable
6. sovereignty
7. Asia, Middle East, Africa
8. ideology, modern societies
9. beliefs, superiority, uniqueness, interest
10. second half of the 18th, World War I

ANSWERS TO MULTIPLE CHOICE QUESTIONS:

l. d   2. d   3. b   4. a   5. b

6. b	7. a	8. d	9. a	10. a
11. c	12.a	13.d	14. b	15. b
16. a	17. c	18. b	19. c	

CHAPTER 13

ANSWERS TO FILL IN THE BLANKS:

A.
1. political parties, Constitutional Convention
2. framework, government
3. limit, procedures, implication
4. rule of law
5. federalism, separation of powers, judicial supremacy, limited government
6. distributing, central
7. Constitution, constitutional
8. bureaucracy, inequity
9. separation of powers
10. checks and balances

B.
1. chief executive, four-year, independent, independent
2. of state, legislator, administrator, diplomat, party leader, commander-in-chief
3. entire nation
4. states
5. Congressional Districts
6. subordinate
7. military, industrial pressure
8. representational, independent
9. constitutionality, acts, state legislatures
10. complex, state, common law
11. lawmaking

ANSWERS TO MULTIPLE CHOICE QUESTIONS:

I. b	2. d	3. a	4. a	5. b
6. b	7. c	8. d	9. c	10. a
11. e	12. a	13. c	14. b	15. c
16. b	17. b			

CHAPTER 14

ANSWERS TO FILL IN THE BLANKS:

A.   l. people
        2. impossible, heterogeneous
        3. pluralism, elitism
        4. pluralists
        5. elitists
        6. opposition
        7. conflict, consensus
        8. take control, conducting
        9. determining and defining, personnel, loyal opposition
       10. two-party system, doctrine, durable

B.   1. lack, democratic
        2. general terms
        3. leaders, active, well educated
        4. 60 percent
        5. young, unskilled, undereducated, minorities
        6. college-educated, professional-managerial, white-collar workers
        7. conventional political participation
        8. political opinion
        9. totality, political
       l0. select, propaganda

ANSWERS TO MULTIPLE CHOICE QUESTIONS:

1. c	2. a	3. b	4. b	5. d
6. c	7. e	8. b	9. d	10. d
11. a	12. c	13. c	14. b	15. c

CHAPTER 15

ANSWERS TO FILL IN THE BLANKS:

A.   1. resources, scarce
        2. what, how, for whom
        3. differently
        4. custom and tradition
        5. command
        6. market, supply and demand
        7. microeconomics

8. decisions
9. utilize, purchasing power, increase, stabilize
10. macroeconomics

B.
1. production
2. land, minerals, water
3. machinery, factories, objects
4. labor, land, capital
5. technology, time, and efficiency
6. versatile
7. finite
8. limited
9. specialization, labor, money
10. mixture, command, market

C.
1. method, attitudes, values
2. workers, machinery
3. large-scale production
4. stock market, co-owners
5. executives, board of directors, stockholders
6. separate
7. legal entity, owners
8. pool
9. oligopoly
10. competition, political, need, quality, management

D.
1. three sectors
2. primary sector
3. secondary sector
4. tertiary sector
5. dramatic changes, sectors
6. primary
7. tertiary
8. professionals, managers, technicians
9. unskilled, semiskilled
10. specialized, theoretical

E.
1. nineteenth
2. Roosevelt
3. increased purchasing power
4. skills
5. industry
6. tertiary

7. foreign, Japan, Western Europe
8. reeducated, disciplined

ANSWERS TO MULTIPLE CHOICE QUESTIONS:

1. b	2. d	3. d	4. c	5. b
6. d	7. a	8. d	9. e	10. d
11. a	12. c	13. d	14. d	15. d

CHAPTER 16

ANSWERS TO FILL IN THE BLANKS:

A.
1. consumers, price
2. households, firms, central authorities
3. abstractions, demand, supply, price
4. product, factor, resource
5. product markets, factor markets
6. withdrawals, injections

B.
1. demand, supply, price
2. energy, labor, money
3. obtains, gives up
4. automatically

C.
1. full employment, mix of output, incomes, price stability, growth
2. policy, taxes
3. fiscal, monetary, direct
4. public expenditures, taxation
5. buying power, private, public
6. affects, redistributes, and growth
7. stabilizer
8. money, credit

ANSWERS TO MULTIPLE CHOICE QUESTIONS:

1. c	2. a	3. d	4. c	5. d
6. e	7. a	8. b	9. c	10. b
11. a	12. c	13. a	14. b	15. e

16. b

CHAPTER 17

ANSWERS TO FILL IN THE BLANKS

A   1. wage and price
     2. depression, inflation, unemployment
     3. goods, services, year
     4. national income, total population
     5. inflated prices, population growth

B.   1. natural, human, capital
     2. restructuring, economy
     3. global
     4. Third World nations, high technology and information
     5. knowledge, data
     6. easier
     7. increase, employer

ANSWERS TO MULTIPLE CHOICE QUESTIONS:

1. d	2. a	3. b	4. d	5. a
6. a	7. c	8. d	9. b	10. e
11. e	12. b	13. c	14. d	15. a
16. d				

CHAPTER 18

A.   1. international relations
     2. conclusions
     3. power, military strength
     4. capacity, affect
     5. national independence, honor, and well-being
     6. competitive, absolute, diffuse, action-oriented, dynamic

B. 1. individuals, psychological factors, specific conditions
    2. general, administrative, crisis
    3. democratic ideology
    4. isolationist, interventionist, internationalist

C. 1. values, roles, instruments
    2. United Nations, foreign aid, collective security
    3. governments
    4. dependable
    5. stretch

D. 1. relative
    2. diplomacy
    3. limited, differences
    4. shifting alliances
    5. become stronger
    6. multipolar, bipolar

ANSWERS TO MULTIPLE CHOICE QUESTIONS:

1. c	2. d	3. d	4. c	5. a
6. c	7. c	8. d	9. b	10. d
11. e	12. b	13. b	14. d	15. c